D1022230

"David Putman authentically shares his life and experiences in *Breaking the Discipleship Code*. Of course we want our churches to be missional; but if we don't break the code of discipleship, our churches will never have the impact God desires. If you lead the disciple-making process of a local church or simply long to be a disciple of Jesus, read *Breaking the Discipleship Code* to discover how to live like Jesus, love like Jesus, and leave behind what Jesus left behind."

Dave Ferguson
Pastor of Community Christian Church,
Cofounder of NewThing Networks, Coauthor of *The Big Idea*

"Some ministry books are so driven by personal stories that the aftertaste is kind of like, 'Interesting stuff, but so what?' Others are so relentlessly practical and tactical that the general tone is cold, sterile, and ultimately forgettable. David has brought the two formats together, drawing simple, practical principles from rich life experience. This book is a must-read for anyone who wants to live a life of strategic impact."

Steven Furtick
Pastor of Elevation Church

"David Putman has laid out a clear vision of what it takes to be a missional follower of Jesus in *Breaking the Discipleship Code*. Using both the teachings of Jesus and real life, he shows us how we can as well."

Bil Cornelius
Pastor of Bay Area Fellowship, Coauthor of *Go Big*

"David Putman has done the church a unique service by writing this book. The lowest common denominator (LCD) for the gospel transforming the world is not the preacher but the disciple. What David advocates in discipleship is so needed today. I am sorry to say there are so few books on the most significant issue of being truly missional: the disciple. This is a must-read."

Bob Roberts Jr.
Pastor of NorthWood Church,
Author of *Transformation*, *Glocalization*, and *The Multiplying Church*

"*Breaking the Discipleship Code* is a timely reminder of our most important task: making disciples. It will help you rethink the way you do discipleship and accomplish the task more effectively."

Mark Batterson
Pastor of National Community Church,
Author of *In a Pit with a Lion on a Snowy Day*

"We don't need good Christians in the classic sense today; we need missional followers of Jesus. By mixing his personal story and sound biblical principles, David draws us into the full life of a follower of Jesus in a variety of real-life contexts. Written with the wisdom of a pastor but the credibility of someone who has to deal with real issues every day, this book will provide great encouragement for your path."

Dave Travis
Managing Director of Leadership Network,
Coauthor of *Beyond Megachurch Myths*

"If you don't want to be challenged to view discipleship in a new and different way, then you had better not read this book. I confess that as I read it I began to re-evaluate my personal walk with Christ. David Putman challenges us not to be who we want to be but to be who Christ wants us to be outside as well as within the body of Christ. I also love his view of the church as being the missionary and not just a sender of missionaries to some other part of the world."

Aubrey Malphurs
Lead Navigator of the Malphurs Group,
Senior Professor of Pastoral Ministries at Dallas Seminary

"In this work, one of my best friends in the world has passionately, carefully, and biblically fired the warning shot for all of us. David beautifully reveals how our Western culture's sin of consumerism has skewed our understanding of what it means to follow Jesus. We must redefine *discipleship* in our Western culture. David does an incredible job of taking us on a journey back to an old and timeless yet new definition of what it really means to follow Jesus. We need to take to heart what he says if we are ever going to see Jesus's mission succeed through us in His church!"

Shawn Lovejoy
Pastor of Mountain Lake Church,
Cofounder of ChurchPlanters.com

"The only way to have a missional church is to have missional people in it. Period. In this engaging volume, David Putman gives wonderful insight into not just describing what missional people look like but how they get that way. It is a great devotional aid for your own personal growth as well as a conversation starter for your group to chart a missional path."

Reggie McNeal
Leadership Network, Author of *Get a Life*

"David Putman clearly understands the nature and calling of God's people, and because of this he has rightly intuited that the missional church at the dawn of the twenty-first century stands or falls on its capacity to make disciples. Here it seems is our next great task. This book is an excellent contribution to that critical cause."

Alan Hirsch
Cofounder of Shapevine.com,
Author of *The Forgotten Ways* and *The Shaping of Things to Come*

"We can talk and dream about missional churches. We can talk and dream about evangelism, worship, and leadership in missional churches. But if we aren't talking about discipleship, the future of missional churches are in big trouble. David invites us into this conversation in this important book."

Dan Kimball
Pastor of Vintage Faith Church,
Author of *They Like Jesus but Not the Church*

BREAKING

the discipleship

CODE

ISBN: 978-0-8054-4676-0

Published by B&H Publishing Group,
Nashville, Tennessee

Dewey Decimal Classification: 248.4
Subject Heading: DISCIPLESHIP \ MISSIONS
EVANGELISTIC WORK

1 2 3 4 5 6 7 8 9 10 11 12 13 14 15   12 11 10 09 08

Becoming a Missional Follower of Jesus

BREAKING

the discipleship

CODE

DAVID PUTMAN

PUBLISHING GROUP

Nashville, Tennessee

||||||||||||||||||||||||||||||||||||||||||||||||||||||||||||||||||||||||||||||||

This book is dedicated to my son Dave,
who recently spent fifteen months in Afghanistan
with the U.S. Army's 82nd Airborne.
Welcome home!

||||||||||||||||||||||||||||||||||||||||||||||||||||||||||||||||||||||||||||||||

Contents

Foreword

*D*avid and I have been friends for a long, long time. Ten years ago, he messed up my life by recruiting me to teach church planting and missions at a seminary and for our mission board. I have seen him in stress, joy, pain, and service. And I have learned a lot from him along the way.

You see, David is like me—an imperfect person. I've seen him lose his temper, act in the flesh, and get focused on the wrong things. (By now you may be wondering what in the world I am doing writing the foreword, but stay with me.)

But I have also seen him as an older brother in the Lord— his spiritual formation and growth exceeding my own. So when I see David, I see someone who understands what it means to be a Christ follower, even when he is fallen and imperfect. I've learned from him, and I want you to as well. Maybe it sounds obvious, but I want to learn discipleship from a disciple, and I have seen that in David— up close; in messy, imperfect, and, yes, God-honoring ways.

In *Breaking the Missional Code,* David and I focused on how a church could be engaged in God's mission by being biblically faithful and engaging people in culture. Our focus was how the church could (and should) be God's missionary in the world.

David has always had a passion for the church, but he also has a passion for God's people being on mission. In *Breaking the*

Discipleship Code, David focuses on what it means to be a missional follower of Jesus.

The book reminds me, a bit, of a book by my friends Thom Rainer and Eric Geiger. In *Simple Church,* Rainer and Geiger call the church back to simplicity. In *Breaking the Discipleship Code,* Putman calls Christians back to simplicity. This book is about rediscovering the centrality of Jesus in your church and everyday life.

Even as I begin a new book exploring our attitudes toward and response to a younger generation, I recognize the importance of this conversation. Becoming a missional follower of Jesus is the key to reaching future generations with the gospel. Over and over again in this book the idea of losing one's religion and finding the Jesus way appears. This is one of the key conversations we need to have as the church. More and more we are finding that while people don't like church, they still like Jesus.

No longer can the church afford to be cute or cool. If we are going to face the challenges ahead of us, we must be real—genuine followers of Christ, living our biblical values and ideas. Being real is about rediscovering the Jesus of our church. It is about opening the doors of our church and letting Him back in. Jesus said, "I stand at the door and knock," while speaking to the church at Laodicea (Rev. 3:20a). David's hope, and my prayer, is that when we focus on following Jesus in the church, He won't have to knock on the outside.

What is a follower of Jesus? How do people become followers of Jesus? What does a missional follower of Jesus look like? These are important questions that find new relevance in today's world. These are not questions that only David needs to address; in today's context, these are questions we must address for ourselves. I think *Breaking the Discipleship Code* will give us insights to help on that journey.

—*Ed Stetzer*
Director, LifeWay Research

Acknowledgments

This book is dedicated to my son, Dave, who spent fifteen months in Afghanistan with the 82nd Airborne. I have learned so much about the freedom I enjoy by watching his relentless spirit and unending sacrifice as he has served on the front lines of the war on terror. I will never take my freedom for granted again. Thank you for your service.

I want to extend a special thank-you to the love of my life, Tami. As my spouse she has gone beyond the call of duty in reading and rereading this manuscript, each time making it better. A special acknowledgment goes to my daughter, whose relentless spirit and the untimely death of her friend, Sam, have taught me so much about living.

Where would I be without Beth Nelson, who has been my friend, creative consultant, editor, and encourager? Thank you for going the extra mile on this. I can't wait to work with you again.

If you read this book, it is obvious that I am what I am because of my parents. I can't express with words what they have meant to me and how they have influenced my life and this book. They are both my heroes, and I am so proud of what Jesus has done in them. They are such strong finishers. I can only hope to be able to keep up with them. They broke the discipleship code long before it was cool to be missional.

A special thanks to the ministry team at Mountain Lake Church that has allowed me to serve alongside them in such a wonderful environment! Mountain Lake has been a lab for *Breaking the Discipleship Code.* I am grateful to Shawn Lovejoy, Chad Ward, Casey Graham, Rodney Anderson, Louie Lovoy, and the rest of the gang at MLC. Marie Lindelli has been off the chart throughout the entire process, working endlessly to handle all the details.

All the people mentioned in this book have done much to impact me and leave God's imprint on my life. Thanks to Larry, Darrin, Gregg, Kevin, Sara, Autumn, Bob, John, and my mom for making the book real by contributing their stories at the end of each chapter in book 3.

I have a special appreciation for Ed Stetzer, my coauthor and friend in writing *Breaking the Missional Code,* which led the way for this book. I am grateful to everyone who read the first book, creating a need for a second book like *Breaking the Discipleship Code.* And finally, thanks to Tom Walters, Robin Patterson, Diana Lawrence, Lisa Parnell, and the rest of the guys and gals at B&H who continue to stick their necks out and take risks on guys like me.

Introduction

My earliest memories of the church consist of serving as an altar boy in a Methodist church. I don't remember how old I was; however, I do know I was old enough to use matches. I hated those darn matches—I had to strike them and then light the long metal tube with a wick at the end. I wasn't sure what that thing was called; I still don't know. I do recall being petrified because it never seemed that those matches would cooperate, and at the same time the entire church was waiting on me to enter the front of the sanctuary. It was a tall order for a mostly unchurched boy whose father was an alcoholic and whose mother was fighting with everything in her to bring a level of normalcy and peace to her four children by hanging on to her Methodist roots.

As a young boy, I found hope in the stories I heard in church. I can remember being drawn to the ones in which the young boys became the heroes: Joseph and his coat of many colors, David as he stood against Goliath, the nameless boy who came to the rescue of the hungry crowd with his two fishes and five loaves of bread. Often I envisioned myself coming to the rescue of my own broken family. I dreamed of what life could be like if God used me to intervene in their lives. I never gave up. I always believed that there was a God in heaven who still delivered little boys from their giants.

The amazing thing is that God heard my prayers. Years passed, and at about the time my childhood prayers began to fade, God delivered me. Actually He delivered us, my entire family. It was Sunday morning, and I still remember it with remarkable clarity. My dad came thundering down the stairs, landing in my room, saying, "Get up, son. We're going to church." Pardon me, I must be dreaming. Could it be that after all these years of praying God had heard and answered my pleas?

That morning, we walked into the church as a family for the first time in years. Even after all this time, I can clearly remember every detail, even down to where we sat: the fourth pew on the left-hand side. That was a really interesting morning. The pastor talked—well, come to think of it, he got up and preached, I mean really preached—about the cultural woes of the day, which happened to be, in our town, men with long hair, women who wore too much makeup, and girls whose skirts were way too short. I can still see my mom sitting to my right tugging on her somewhat short skirt. I thought it was really cool that we were all in church together, but it was also a very uncomfortable experience.

To our collective surprise, we went back the next week, only this time we were much more prepared. My mom had let out the hems of all of my sisters' dresses, she wore considerably less makeup, and my hair had a nice military feel to it. The amazing and ironic thing about the whole experience was that my dad was the only one who didn't have to change anything about his appearance. Yet at the same time, he was the one furthest from God, assuming distance from God is measured by behaviors, like alcohol consumption, fighting, womanizing, cheating, and the like.

This whole experience is what I consider our first conversion. We were converted not necessarily to faith but to the specific church culture of that day. With longer hems, less makeup, and shorter hair, we were now candidates for spiritual conversion. Within a few weeks, our entire family proceeded to the front of the church during the formal invitation to commit, convert, rededicate, join, or accept the call to preach. In that church culture, the end of the service was always reserved for a formal invitation to do one or more of those things. For my family that day, we took one of nearly each commitment (though none of us accepted a call to pastorship that particular day). That night, as a family, we experienced an *oikos* conversion—the kind that sweeps through a family in a Holy Spirit kind of way. In essence, we began a spiritual journey that would take years for all of us to figure out.

Today, not only are my parents still together, they love each other dearly. My dad has been a pastor for more than thirty years, mostly in one church, and my mom has been a real champion in living life to the fullest in Jesus. My dad is not only devoted to the Lord, he is devoted to Mom. When I ask him about his life of devotion and service to her, he humbly responds, "Son, when I look at all Jesus has done in my life and everything I put your mom through the first part of our life together, I sort of figure that nothing is too good for her." Jesus really does make a difference. I'm still amazed after all these years how faithful God has been to a little boy with a dream for his family.

I tell this story for a number of reasons. One is because I want to paint a picture of the religious culture that introduced my family and me to Jesus. In that time and in that place, there wasn't a lot of discrepancy between church culture and secular culture. That is much of the reason that my dad, even though he was far from Jesus, didn't require a conversion to church culture before he experienced a conversion to Jesus.

Today's secular culture is quite different. Not only does the church have little authority in the life of the average person, it is not uncommon to meet someone who has no experience at all in the church. We can no longer assume that people know who Moses was or what the Ten Commandments are. People who are outside the church, as my family was, view the church mostly as boring, irrelevant, narrow, misinformed, weird, odd, out-of-date, judgmental, and any number of other choice adjectives. This is probably not new information to you. What may surprise you is that they don't know who Jesus is. I don't mean they don't understand His love or His gift of salvation; I mean they actually don't know His name. Several years ago, I introduced a little girl to Him at a campground where I worked. She was so excited to have invited Jesus into her life that when her parents came to pick her up, she ran to them shouting, "Mom! Dad! I just invited God's Son . . ." Pausing, she looked at me and said, "What's His name?" I told her, and she continued her pronouncement, "Yeah, that's it; I just invited Jesus into my life!"

Many people today are on spiritual journeys, but they are far removed from Christ and the church. They believe in God, but they are not sure exactly which gods they believe in. The church exists within hostile territory, and the Christian faith is seen as oppressive, narrow, and bigoted. Those who embrace Jesus, instead of being embraced and celebrated by their family, coworkers, and communities, are often ostracized by those closest to them. Welcome to our new spiritual frontier. In gods we trust.

I grew up during a time when it wasn't too much to ask people to convert to church culture before they converted to Christ. The distance between those two, in many communities, was insignificant. However, the home-court advantage we once enjoyed as the church no longer exists, and as a result, we are a missional people called to a world where the rules of engagement have changed. This change caught many of us off guard. If we are perfectly honest with ourselves, we no longer know how to engage the world with the gospel; instead we hunker down where it is safe. We have created our own Christian culture of isolation, characterized by our own schools, TV shows, coffee shops, colleges, networks, sports leagues, and entertainment parks. We have become islands unto ourselves. It's not that we don't believe in the Great Commandment or the Great Commission, or that we don't like people who are disconnected from Christ; we simply don't know what to do to escape from our islands.

This book is about bursting our religious bubbles and engaging the world. We can no longer look at missions as something we accomplish in a foreign country. The mission field has come home, and we are right in the middle of it. This book will help you become that missionary to your own culture, to become a missional follower of Jesus. It is about recognizing that we are still "the salt of the earth" and "the light of the world" (Matt. 5:13a, 16a). At the same time, I recognize that somewhere over the past couple of decades our world has changed, and the Christian faith no longer enjoys widespread acceptance as it may once have. Most of us no longer know how to navigate the world as God's missionary people and His missionary church, yet there still is a deep moving of God's Spirit in His people and church. We are hungry for God's power and movement in and through us, and we are ready to release the religious traditions we have employed for tradition's sake. We simply need permission and perspective for making this bold journey.

Therefore, this book is about our need to rethink years of cultural Christianity that, more often than we want to admit, stands in the way of those outside of Christ. Simply put, some of us were equipped to live the Christian life in a different time and a different age. If you recently entered the church for the first time, you may feel the tension; if you've been in church for many years, you may be the tension. I want to call us as followers of Jesus to surrender "the way we've always done it" for the sake of those for whom that way hasn't done anything.

In the three parts of this book, I want to answer questions that will form a framework for rethinking and ultimately reliving the

Christian life: What is a missional follower of Jesus? How does a person become a missional follower of Jesus? And what does a missional follower of Jesus look like in different cultural contexts?

In part 1, I want to strip down the faith to its bare essence. After years of piling on traditions and unrealistic expectations, let's slough all that away and examine the lives of Jesus and of His disciples. Crucial to obeying Jesus's command to make disciples (Matt. 28:19) is an understanding of what it means to be a follower of Jesus who is determined to take that glorious light into the world.

In the second section, we will focus on how people become missional followers of Jesus. Here's a hint: Guilt-driven altar calls and forceful explanations of the four spiritual laws aren't necessarily a one-size-fits-all solution. The radical changes that have affected our culture in recent decades require that we, as followers of Jesus, amend our methods of evangelism, all the while holding tightly to the truth of Jesus.

Finally, in the third part of this book, I want to challenge you to leave your comfort zone and go missional, taking the message of Jesus into the world. Answer these questions for yourself and for your own cultural context: What does a missional follower of Jesus look like? What does he or she do in different situations? How does a missional follower of Jesus respond to the world?

Writing this book has been a journey for me and my family and one that has not been easy. However, in the process of the journey, I have learned much about Jesus, more than I ever expected. I set out to write a book about "breaking the discipleship code," about helping followers of Jesus find effective ways to bring others to Him. It was and still is my hope that people who read *Breaking the Missional Code* (which I coauthored with Ed Stetzer) will find this book a helpful companion in their ministries and their lives. I hope to challenge every reader to escape his or her comfort zone and explore the invigoration that comes with discipling others. In truth, I did not anticipate that I would break the discipleship code for myself, but about three-quarters into the writing of this book, God began to grip my heart in a new way, giving me fresh insight into discipleship.

I realized that through the years I have acquired a lot of unnecessary religious baggage. Most of it I don't even recognize in myself—it's always more apparent to me on someone else. However, writing this book brought me face-to-face with the image in the mirror, and I've gained a whole new perspective about myself. For me, becoming a missional follower of Jesus means losing my religion: letting go of those "religious" things I do simply because I think followers of Jesus are supposed to do them, because "that's the way it's always been." But it's not simply about letting go of religion. More importantly, I realized that I must connect with Jesus in a new way, a simpler way, the way the apostles did by examining His life.

For me, I am going to be satisfied to live the rest of my life as a follower of Jesus and Jesus alone. I hope you will too. It is my prayer that you will lose your religion and find the Jesus way.

Book 1

What Is a Follower of Jesus?

If all the volumes written about what it means to be a follower of Jesus had to be reduced to three words, my three words would be *live, love,* and *leave.* As a matter of fact, I believe it would be helpful to think of it in such simple terms. Jesus exploded onto the gospel scene with these radical words: "Repent, for the kingdom of heaven is near" (Matt. 4:17b). Repent? I can hear the Pharisees now: "What are we repenting of?" They were the most religious people in the history of organized religion. Not only did they abide by the Ten Commandments, they added 613 rules and regulations to ensure they obeyed every detail of the Law. Yet Jesus began His earthly ministry in this context—telling them to repent. Can you imagine their consternation? Can you envision their faces? We know from the Gospels that they were appalled at this man who was telling them to repent of their religion for religion's sake. He was about to show them a whole new way.

I can't help but believe that if Jesus began His ministry today, He would begin it exactly the same way: "Repent, for the kingdom of heaven is near." Like the Pharisees, we think we have it all down. We have our rules, regulations, cultural norms, and moral standards of conduct. We have our devotional guides, disciplines, doctrines, values, mission statements, and religious practices. I can imagine Him saying, "Hold on, guys. This is not what I had in mind. You are doing a lot of good stuff, but you have forgotten Me. Open up the door. I'm standing here knocking. Can't you hear Me?"

That's exactly why I think describing what it means to be a missional follower of Jesus in three words is a good exercise. What does it mean to live like Christ, love like Christ, and leave what Christ left behind? Is that not the essence of what Jesus did when He burst on the scene in Matthew 4 and told Peter and John, "Come, follow me, and I will make you to become fishers of men" (v. 19)? Is that not the essence of what He called Matthew to when He simply spoke the words, "Follow me," in Matthew 9:9? Jesus was inviting them to live His way.

Do not be mistaken: Jesus did not come to form a religion. He came into a religious world in order to transcend religions and invite us to a relationship with Him. With that in mind, let me invite you on a journey of rethinking. What if we could simplify things to such an extent that our faith was stripped down to a relationship? I think it can be done! For the next three chapters, forget everything you think you know and focus on a simple definition and a simple way of life that allows us to become followers of Jesus in the purest form. To live, to love, and to leave is a profound yet simple way of living that brings us back to the core of what it means to be a follower of Jesus.

"Come to me, all you who are weary and burdened, and I will give you rest. Take my yoke upon you and learn from me, for I am gentle and humble in heart, and you will find rest for your souls. For my yoke is easy and my burden is light."

—MATTHEW 11:28–30

CHAPTER 1

Live as Jesus Lived

In 1989, I had one of those moments with God that turned my life inside out and upside down. I was attending a church conference in Mission Viejo, California, and I witnessed the ministry of a young man named Rick Warren who was in the process of breaking the missional code in his community. It didn't take long to realize that God had special plans for this pastor. There God spoke very loudly and clearly into my life; all I knew was that I wanted my life to count.

I went home and for the first time wrote out a life mission statement: "My mission is to discover true freedom in Christ and to help as many people as possible do likewise." Since that time, I have been on a journey to discover what it really means to live like Jesus. At that time, I was in bondage, wrestling with strong emotions from earlier times in my life and coping with serious religious baggage. As a pastor, I lived under the pressure of meeting the expectations of the people I led, the pastors I knew, and the denomination I was connected with. You know that pressure as well. I didn't know the yoke that Jesus described as "easy." My yoke was heavy and hard.

Since 1989, this journey has taken me to places I never envisioned going. First and foremost, it has taken me closer to finding the true freedom in Christ that I longed for. I feel what Paul must have felt when he wrote the words, "I'm not saying that I have this all together, that I have it made. But I am well on my way, reaching out for Christ, who has so wondrously reached out for me. Friends, don't get me wrong: by no means do I count myself an expert in all of this, but I've got my eye on the goal, where God is beckoning us onward—to Jesus. I'm off and running, and I'm not turning back" (Phil. 3:12–14 MSG).

I've learned that there is more to being a follower of Jesus than culture and behavior. It is easy to describe our relationship with God based on the works we do and the actions we take. It is even easy to assume that we are good Christians as long as we are involved in a local church, attend worship, engage in Bible studies and prayer services, tithe, and serve on a volunteer committee or two. If you are really honest, you know people who do all of the right things but at the same time are some of the meanest people in the world. They lack fruit. Nothing about their life and character has anything to do with Christ.

What does it mean to be a follower of Jesus? I love the way Jesus Himself answered this question: "Come to me, all you who are weary and burdened, and I will give you rest. Take my yoke upon you and learn from me, for I am gentle and humble in heart and you will find rest for your souls. For my yoke is easy and my burden is light" (Matt. 11:28–30). Talk about freedom! This verse is liberating! In Jesus's time, the "yoke" was a certain teaching, what a teacher taught his disciples. The Pharisees had a teaching, but it was difficult to follow and was accompanied by a heavy burden. It was controlling and impossible to live under. On the other hand, Jesus had a different yoke, a different teaching. It was easy and liberating because it was focused on who He was rather than on who the follower was trying to be. And for even more good news, this way that Jesus offered was a radical way of life He invites us all into.

To Know Him

The Gospel of John ends, "Jesus did many other things as well. If every one of them were written down, I suppose that even the whole world would not have room for the books that would be written" (21:25). It is impossible to speak in detail about how to live as Jesus lived, but you can be certain that in order to follow Him, you have to know Him. And I mean really, really know Him well. Jesus spent nearly three years in intimate relationships with His disciples. They heard His call and they followed Him. They lived life together. They ate together, fought together, debated together, and experienced both hardship and joy together. They went everywhere together. They knew what He cared about, how He would handle different situations, and what was important to Him. They knew how He loved the Father and loved His neighbor as Himself. They knew that His life was marked by sacrifice and purpose. They understood that He was on a mission and that people mattered to Him. The disciples knew His ways intimately.

How do you boil down all of His teachings into one simple truth that serves as a rock-hard foundation for living as He lived? Perhaps the best description is found in Philippians 2:5–8: "Your attitude should be the same as that of Christ Jesus: Who, being in very nature God, did not consider equality with God something to be grasped, but made himself nothing, taking the very nature of a servant, being made in human likeness. And being found in appearance as a man, he humbled himself and become obedient to death—even death on a cross."

If you pay attention to these verses, they give important insight into the life Jesus called His followers to live. Paul answered the question, "What does it mean to live as Jesus lived?" Notice what was happening here. No one took Jesus's life; He laid it down voluntarily. Did you notice the progression of events? Jesus has existed for eternity in heaven with God the Father, His equal. He chose to be born on earth in order to become a servant and to sacrifice Himself for the redemption of all mankind. Each step along the way took Him deeper into a sort of downward mobility that seems foreign to our way of life today. While we are constantly looking for how we can move up, get ahead, and break out in front of the pack, Jesus continued to surrender more and more of Himself until, ultimately, He gave up His own life.

Jesus was not the only one who understood this. Perhaps you remember John the Baptist, a relative of Jesus and known as the forerunner of Christ. Great crowds of people followed John the Baptist, and many of them even mistook him for the Messiah. Once Jesus appeared on earth, many of those who had followed John began to follow Jesus. We are told that many who formerly followed John came to Jesus to be baptized, and this raised concerns with John's disciples. When they approached John about this, he replied by saying, "He [Jesus] must increase, but I must decrease" (John 3:30 KJV).

Downward Mobility

To me, that verse explains exactly what it means to live as Jesus lived. We are to decrease to ourselves on a daily basis in order that Jesus might increase in our lives. More of Jesus, less of me! We lose our lives in order to find His way.

My good friends Larry and Susan understand this better than almost anyone I know. I had the honor of working with Larry in the late 1990s after Larry left his dream church and his season tickets to the Tennessee Volunteers (which I understand is equivalent to giving away your birthright if you are from Tennessee) to join our organization. He felt called to something bigger that required him to become smaller. It was a very difficult move that required a significant amount of self-sacrifice. Not long after Larry arrived in our organization, it became apparent that this act of sacrifice was only the beginning of his intentional downward mobility. Over the next few years, I watched God work in Larry's life as he chose to live in an apartment instead of buying a large brick house in the suburbs. He made radical adjustments to his lifestyle simply because he sensed a need to be prepared for whatever God wanted to do in his life.

It wasn't long until Larry and Susan felt confirmed that their calling was to leave everything familiar and move to a new country to plant churches. During this transition their intentional downward mobility became even more obvious. Over the next few months, I watched Larry and Susan sell nearly everything they owned: two cars, their furniture, their home, and almost everything inside it. Before they left on this new journey, Larry could literally fit everything he owned into one crate. Even their kids had reduced all of their possessions down to a box each.

On the last day Larry was in our office, he called our team into his office where only a few treasured possessions remained. He distributed these possessions among each and every member of our team. He gave one person a picture of the University of Tennessee Volunteers National Championship football team that hung on his office wall. He gave me a signed print of Lost Mountain, Georgia, the place where our lives first became intertwined and where Larry planted his first church. He gave away pictures of his kids to a couple of ladies in exchange for their commitment to pray for them. When everything was gone, we all joined hands, prayed, cried, and said our good-byes. Now it was official: Larry had nothing material left and was off on a bold new adventure to follow the call of Jesus.

We live as Jesus lived when we begin to experience this intentional downward mobility, making ourselves nothing, as Paul said. When this happens, we discover full access to His kingdom, and as we enter His kingdom, we come to experience a whole new way of life. Lately I've found a number of people who have a lot in common with Larry and Susan. Not too long ago, I talked with a good friend who told me he had reached all of his professional goals as well as his goals for providing for his family. He has a wonderful wife and children, a nice home, a substantial income, and many wonderful relationships. He is truly living the American dream. Yet at the same time, he is living in tension with what has come to be really important to him. He feels called to follow Jesus in a radical way and to live as Jesus lived. It occurred to me as we spoke that my friend would spend the rest of his life working out this whole idea of being downwardly mobile. Sure, he has reached his goals, but often, reaching his goals has come with a great price. He realized that what he thought he wanted, by the time he attained it, wasn't actually what he needed.

Now, I am watching him go through a process similar to Larry and Susan's experience. I see him consistently and intentionally decreasing his hold on this life in order that Jesus might increase in his life. I am thankful that these types of journeys have become familiar to me, and it brings me immeasurable joy to see them played out among people I care about. I can only imagine the joy it brings our God! It is the journey that must become familiar to all of us if we are to follow Jesus in an authentic way. It is a journey for which we must be ready to reexamine everything we think we know.

Inside Out, Not Outside In

It is easy to look at the things we own or have achieved and assume that these things are the measure of a good life. We some-times believe that the more we achieve or accomplish, the closer we come to arriving at a certain status in life and the more peace, meaning, and acceptance we will experience. We often assume that these things are associated with the life Jesus wants for us, only to discover they are, in fact, temporary. Be encouraged—it's not a new struggle. The religious scholars and teachers of Jesus's time felt this as well. We buy into the idea that if we can master a moral code, Jesus will commend us for having lived a good life. This is a fallacy, and it is dangerous to believe. Jesus called the most morally correct people of his day hypocrites, blind guides, snakes, a brood of vipers, and whitewashed tombs (see Matt. 23:1–39). Ouch!

On another occasion when questioned by the Pharisees, He told them, "The kingdom of God does not come visibly, nor will people say, 'Here it is,' or 'There it is,' because the kingdom of God is within you" (Luke 17:21). These words were indeed counter-cultural to the religious world of His day, and they still are today. As we live as Jesus lived, we may find the most turbulent times on the outside, but deep within ourselves we discover both the purpose and the peace of God. We learn that life isn't about us, and therefore we begin to view our lives with a different perspective.

Upside Down, Not Right Side Up

I often wonder, *If Jesus were on the earth today, would I recognize Him?* I walk down the aisles of the stores where I shop, and I'm afraid that if Jesus looked like many of the people I see there, I probably would not have a lot to do with Him. Isn't it amazing that we sometimes put Jesus into our own neat little boxes, assuming that He would act, speak, look, and think as we do? Instead of adjusting our lives to emulate His, we create a Jesus that accommodates our own choices and lifestyles. We will do nearly anything to justify our choices and our way of life.

We sometimes think it's interesting how radical Jesus's message was in His day, but if we examine ourselves, I think we'll find that it doesn't make a whole lot of sense today either. Read the passage of Scripture we refer to as the Beatitudes in Matthew 5. Jesus called them "blessed" who were poor in spirit, who mourned, or were meek or persecuted. You won't find this ideology in a lot of leadership or self-help books. Jesus taught that the greatest among us would be the least, and the last would ultimately be first. He raised up the humble. He sat a child in His lap as an example of greatness. At times He completely ignored the religious leaders of His day, and at other times He took them to task with a vengeance. He led from the back and served from the front. He modeled in every way that to really experience life, we have to give it away to others.

Great Big, Not Itty-Bitty

Frankly, we often live our lives as if we were at the center of all things, but our world becomes itty-bitty when it becomes all about us. What we learn by living like Jesus is that He considered others at the center of the world, and He knew how big the world truly was. He held what was huge in His very hands, and at the same time was in intimate contact with every little detail.

Nothing went unnoticed to Jesus. He felt the woman with the hemorrhage as she brushed by Him in a massive rush of people, and He also saw the crowds who came to hear Him teach and was moved with compassion because He knew they were like sheep with no shepherd. At one time He fed the five thousand and another time had a touching supper with the Twelve. He called His disciples to come follow Him one by one and at the same time held the world in His hand. He died on the cross for the sins of all people for all time, but while dying, He had an evocative conversation with a thief crucified beside Him.

Jesus came demonstrating that it is in no way all about us. This is not our little world, but rather we are citizens of His kingdom; and His kingdom is like a mustard seed that grows to the most magnificent proportion.

In John 3:16 we read that God so loved the world that He gave us His Son. Yes, it's true He loves me, but I am not the main attraction. He loves the whole world. He loves street gangs. He loves strippers. He loves AIDS victims in Zambia. He is really concerned about the genocide in the Sudan. He pays attention to every conflict and every battle. His heart breaks for the injustices we fail to see. Yet, in far too rare moments, He peels back the veneer of my self-centeredness and allows me to feel His compassion for the world. He did it recently when I placed a pair of shoes on the hard, calloused feet of a ten-year-old in Jamaica. I think it was a first for both of us.

God cares about the hungry, the oppressed, the misdirected, and the disconnected. He cares about His world: world hunger, world AIDS, and world peace. He cares about you and me and even our pettiest of concerns. He invites us to His dream of peace on earth and goodwill toward all men. He invites us to join Him in His prayer, "Your kingdom come, your will be done on earth as it is done in heaven" (Matt. 6:10). To live as Jesus lived is to pray as Jesus prayed. Let Your kingdom come on earth in my life, in my environment, in my experience, and in my purpose as it is in heaven.

Simple, Not Complex

Even with the chaos of the world around us, it is still amazing to me that our lives can become so complicated. I think of my parents' home, where they have four storage buildings filled with the things they have accumulated over the years. I was picking through them recently, looking for a few usable pieces of furniture for my daughter. I left that day promising them that I would return to take time to go through their stuff, thinking to myself that much of it should be hauled off to the garbage dump. It occurred to me that this is a good picture of how we accumulate so much stuff we don't need and hang on to for years. Before we know it, our lives are filled with trash because we're too afraid to throw it away, too afraid of what might happen if it weren't around when we needed it.

I think the same is true for our relationship with Jesus. We begin this journey of following Jesus with simple, childlike faith. We are a lot like the blind man—all we know is that once we were blind, but now we see. Coming to know Jesus and following Him are pure joy because we are focused solely on this loving relationship with our Savior.

Yet over time we begin to "supplement" that relationship with other things—things that really don't have anything to do with Jesus, things we think we need because, on some level, we're afraid that a time will come when Jesus won't be enough and we'll need those other things to support us. What was once simple becomes inordinately complex. But Jesus calls us to return to Him in simplicity, abandon our excess, and come to Him again as a child.

The Jesus Way

Yet we must be careful that when we talk of simplicity, it is not merely for the sake of simplicity. It is simplicity for the sole purpose of rediscovering the Jesus way of life. It is saying no to religion in order to say yes to Jesus. Where do we begin this journey of living as Jesus lived? In the early days of my encounters with Jesus, I had a Bible with all the words of Jesus written in red. I loved this Bible. I remember, as a thirteen-year-old, discovering Jesus through that Bible for the first time. I would read the red with a hunger for understanding. I was in love with Jesus, and somehow I knew intuitively that the key to my relationship with Him was in reading His words. I fell in love with the Jesus of the Bible and wanted to know and emulate everything about Him.

Living as Jesus lived is about coming to know Jesus personally through experience. It's about coming to know Him through the lenses of the gospel and the presence of His very Spirit; it's about a journey of friendship. It's about living life to the maximum by living minimally. It's about giving up to ultimately go up. It's about laying down in order to be lifted up. It's about becoming last only to find yourself first. It's about decreasing in order to see Him increase. Living as Jesus lived is a new way of life that requires rethinking all our assumptions, opinions, expectations, and experiences about the kingdom. Jesus descended in order to ultimately ascend, and so must we.

Something to Think About

1. What religious baggage needs to be eliminated from your life?
2. If living as Jesus lived involves intentional downward mobility, what does this look like in your life?
3. What does it mean for you to live as Jesus lived?

"'Love the Lord your God with all your heart and with all your soul and with all your mind and with all your strength. . . . Love your neighbor as yourself.' There is no commandment greater than these."
—MARK 12:30–31

CHAPTER 2

Love as Jesus Loved

Let's return to my definition of what it means to be a follower of Jesus, which is to live as Jesus lived, to love as Jesus loved, and to leave what Jesus left behind. None of these can stand alone. If you live as Jesus lived without the love, you reduce what it means to be a follower of Jesus to a set of disciplines, rules, and routines. Was this not already done by a certain group called the Pharisees? Closely following the life of Jesus becomes a model for how we are to live, but that alone is not enough. When our motivations are wrong, regardless of how we live, everything is wrong. Paul certainly understood this when he spoke these words: "If I speak in the tongues of men and of angels, but have not love, I am only a resounding gong or a clanging cymbal. If I have the gift of prophecy and can fathom all mysteries and all knowledge, and if I have a faith that can move mountains, but have not love, I am nothing. If I give all I possess to the poor and surrender my body to the flames, but have not love, I gain nothing" (1 Cor. 13:1–3).

When we love like Jesus, we are compelled to live like Jesus. Therefore, it is important that we go no further until we have spent time pondering His love and how this love shows up in our lives.

A Divine Romance

I've learned so much about love from my wife, Tami, and from the experiences we have shared throughout our lives together. I think our temptation, when describing Christian love, is to reduce it to a few expressions of affection. But what does it mean to really love as Jesus loved? If living as Jesus lived is about intentional downward mobility, then I propose that loving as Jesus loved is about a story of divine romance. To explain, let me invite you into my marriage, for it is in this romance that I have learned much about Jesus's love for me.

Once in a while something comes our way that, though uninvited, has the most peculiar way of turning our upside-down world right side up. For me this moment was on January 21, 2003, at approximately 7:30 p.m. The next morning, long before the rooster crowed, I would be headed to the airport for another of my frequent trips to New York. Tami and I decided to spend a little time together by going for a jog in our neighborhood. As we took the first turn off our street, it began to rain, and we decided to return to the house. As Tami jogged about fifteen yards ahead of me, I noticed a fast-moving van trying to navigate the turn in front of us. In the moments that followed, everything seemed surreal. All at once, each moment measured an eternity, and each moment passed at a lightning pace. But as I tried to warn Tami, I saw and heard the impact of the van striking my wife of twenty-three years.

The van came to a screeching stop. In my attempt to process what I had seen and rush to her aid, I remember having three very concise thoughts at that same surreal speed: (1) that I had just lost my wife, (2) that I wasn't sure I could handle what I was going to see when I got to her, and (3) that I was probably going to have to tell my son and daughter that they had lost their mom.

As I made my way around the van, I heard the most horrifying, yet sweetest sound of my life. Tami was crying out in pain. As I scanned her injuries, it became clear that they were mostly isolated to her lower extremities. As far as I could tell, there was no trauma to her head or upper body. She was alive.

The surreal passage of time that was at once painfully slow and lightning quick lasted for twenty-four hours following the accident. Two of my pastors showed up at the hospital. I called Tami's parents and said, "First of all, she's OK, but Tami was hit by a van." I canceled my trip to New York, and the people I worked with streamed through the hospital, one after the other. What I remember with the most clarity is the next evening. It was finally quiet, and Tami and I were all alone. Tami was resting with a little help from the morphine that pumped through her body, my daughter had gone home, Tami's surgery was scheduled for the next day, and I sat there alone with the weight of what had happened slowly moving in. As I sat next to the hospital bed, I began making my way through my e-mails, now a day old, on my Blackberry. Buried in the dozens I had received was one that stood out. It was from Tami, written only a few hours before the accident, and it read, "I love you; I can't wait to spend time with you tonight." I couldn't hold back the tears any longer, and I wept. It was the kind of big, silent weeping that shakes your body, but no sound comes out. The words "I love you" ricocheted off my soul and found their way into the deepest, fullest part of my heart. I, too, was in love.

Helping and serving Tami during her recovery was truly a labor of love. Every small step was something we could not help but celebrate: getting out of the house for the first time, shopping in a wheelchair, using crutches for the first time, moving upstairs, crawling up and down our steps, getting around with a walker, taking a bath without a shower seat, and taking those first steps with no crutches or walker. Our senses were heightened. God was in every detail, and life was in full bloom in our souls.

Totally Impractical

During this time I begin to think about how I could show Tami in a very tangible way how much I loved her. How can I love her as Jesus loved? With our twenty-fifth wedding anniversary coming up, I decided to give her the diamond ring I had always wanted her to have but could never afford. About eighteen months before our anniversary, I headed off on the quest to find the perfect diamond for the love of my life. Sure enough, before long I found the perfect stone for her. It was absolutely amazing—clear, bright, flawless, and perfect. Until I saw the price tag. However, as I shopped for less expensive diamonds, nothing else would suffice. I had found the perfect diamond. Along with this perfect diamond, I had found an antique band detailed with etching that set off the other diamonds. It was beautiful, yet at the same time it was obscenely expensive and extremely impractical.

As I contemplated this impractical expression of love, I simply couldn't get away from it. The thought of working hard over the next eighteen months to earn extra money, of making daily sacrifices to save for the gift, motivated me even more. One Sunday morning as I sat in church, I admit that I'm not sure what the pastor was teaching about because I was having a serious conversation with God about the ring. Should I go ahead and purchase it, or is it simply too impractical?

I was reminded of the passage of Scripture in which Mary gave Jesus a gift just as impractical: "Mary took about a pint of pure nard, an expensive perfume; she poured it on Jesus' feet and wiped his feet with her hair. And the house was filled with the fragrance of the perfume. . . . Judas Iscariot, who was later to betray him, objected, 'Why wasn't this perfume sold and the money given to the poor? It was worth a year's wages.' . . . 'Leave her alone,' Jesus replied. 'It was meant that she should save this perfume for the day of my burial. You will always have the poor among you, but you will not always have me'" (John 12:3–8).

Wow! Mary took a bottle of very expensive perfume, broke the bottle, and poured it over His feet, wiping them with her hair. What could be more impractical or seemingly wasteful? It occurred to me then that God's love is best demonstrated through His impractical gift of Jesus. In John 3:16, we read, "'For God so loved the world that he gave his one and only Son, that whoever believes in him shall not perish but have eternal life.'" Many of us who grew up with some kind of familiarity with the church have read and memorized this Scripture again and again. It is part of our Christian vocabulary, sometimes the only Bible verse a person knows by heart. But take a moment to think about what it really says: "God so loved the world."

Sometimes, I don't love the world. When I think of my son, a soldier who risked his life daily in Afghanistan, I don't love that part of the world. When my daughter tells me about an injustice she has experienced at the hand of a careless and thoughtless person, I don't love the world. When the guy in front of me cuts me off because he is too busy talking on his cell phone to notice, I don't love the world. Yet God so loved the world, all of it, that He gave his one and only Son to save it. Now that's impractical.

Impractical Expression

Recently my daughter came home with a tattoo on her back that displayed the words of Jesus written in Greek: "Father, forgive them, for they know not what they do." Once the initial shock wore off, I imagined Jesus on the cross and those who had placed Him there, mocking and brutalizing Him from below. And His response was, "Father, forgive them." Totally impractical!

Move ahead two thousand years to my nineteen-year-old daughter, recently deeply hurt by a relationship. She's coming to terms with that hurt through the lovely example of Jesus in His darkest hour when, at the hands of His executioners, He pronounced a blessing on those who were working fervently to kill Him. When I asked her why a tattoo, but more importantly why this specific verse, she responded, "You know I've struggled with this for so long, and I've been thinking—life is short. I don't want to be angry anymore, and this tattoo reminds me of this." Wow! Maybe I need a tattoo that reminds me of the same thing. Maybe we all need a tattoo.

Impractical Instruction

Is this what loving as Jesus loved is all about? That is, extending forgiveness to those who have deeply hurt us? Perhaps we can take a lesson from Jesus's Sermon on the Mount. Talk about impracticality: "If someone strikes you on the right check, turn to him the other also. And if someone wants to sue you and take your tunic, let him have your cloak as well. If someone forces you to go one mile, go with him two miles. Give to the one who asks you, and do not turn away from the one who wants to borrow from you" (Matt. 5:39b–42). If that wasn't enough, Jesus went on to say, "But I tell you: Love your enemies and pray for those who persecute you, that you may be sons of your Father in heaven" (Matt. 5:44–45a).

Jesus was preaching to a crowd who understood oppression. These people were, even as Jesus spoke, subject to the rule of Rome in addition to the regional and local laws under which their money could be taken without receiving anything in return. Yet as Jesus explained His way of living, the best way, the way of God, He instructed them to turn over everything they had with love and a generous spirit. Completely impractical!

Impractical Place

I saved for months, and finally the day came when I was to give Tami the ring. I knew the place had to be perfect for such an extravagant gift. Perhaps a trip to a vineyard was in order or to our favorite restaurant, or maybe we could fly to New York City so I could give it to her on top of the Empire State Building. Then it occurred to me—the perfect place to give her this expression of my love was at our own house. My mind returned to the garden at the back of our house we had built together, the Eden we had made with our own hands. It was the place where we had fought, loved, laughed, and cried. It was a place where we had prayed and discussed the challenges and the joys of our lives.

After she returned home from a trip, I invited her to join me in our garden, where I began by describing the beginning of our life together and went on to tell her how much she meant to me. I shared with her the many wonderful characteristics that made her uniquely her. I talked about the fun times in our lives and how I admired her more than anyone in this world for the ways she handled the most difficult things. I celebrated her recovery from the accident and thanked God for sparing her life and giving me many more years with her. I talked about how she fulfilled my heart and my life. I wept and she wept with me, and then I pulled out this totally impractical expression of love and placed it on her finger. Even it paled in comparison to the love we have come to know and experience.

Tami and I now find ourselves in an interesting place along our journey together. She has almost fully recovered from the accident, and after one week in the hospital, surgery to rebuild her shattered leg, three months of being nonambulatory, and countless hours of sheer determination, Tami only occasionally shows outward signs of her injury. Throughout this and other, sometimes painful, life experiences, we are discovering what it means to follow Jesus and, in doing so, to love what He loves.

Jesus's love is the most amazing love you can ever imagine. It is this love that motivates us to live as He lived and to respond in sometimes irrational ways. It is a love that makes no sense, that keeps on loving no matter what. It is a love we never fully obtain, but we always pursue. It is a love that contains the secret to life.

Something to Think About

1. What are impractical ways you have loved others as Jesus has loved you?

2. Who are specific people in your life who need to be loved as Jesus loved?

3. Describe your plans for loving them in this way.

*Jesus went up into the hills and called to him those he wanted,
and they came to him. He appointed twelve—designating them
apostles—that they might be with him and that he might send
them out to preach and to have authority to drive out demons.*

—MARK 3:13–15

CHAPTER 3

Leave What Jesus Left Behind

Recently, I received an e-mail from someone from my past that read, "Is this David Putman, the son of J. D. Putman?" When I verified the sender's assumption, the reply was, "I should have known it was when I saw you investing in young pastors. The fruit doesn't fall far from the tree."

This person had run across a ministry I cofounded and colead; ChurchPlanters.com is designed to mentor and coach young church planters. I smiled inwardly, as for the first time I connected the dots between my dad's life and ministry and my own. It struck me as funny because it had never occurred to me that my life was a product of my dad's legacy of investing in younger pastors. He never developed a specific program or founded a ministry or intense discipleship process; he simply follows his heart and does what comes naturally to him by helping others.

He recently underwent surgery, and once again I was reminded of how he lives and loves. When I arrived in his hospital room, four guys, pastors and laymen he continues to pour his life into, were attending to his needs during his recovery. I remembered my dad telling me once that when he was a younger pastor struggling to get started, he had to do it mostly on his own, and at that point he decided if he ever had the chance, he would devote time to helping other young pastors.

Regardless of whether you are a pastor, businessperson, teacher, doctor, student, or stay-at-home mom, or hold any other title, you can make that same decision to spend your life investing in other people. For me, that means living like Jesus, loving like Jesus, and leaving what Jesus left behind—more followers of Jesus. He did this by living His life in close association with others and by investing in their lives. That's the commitment we all must make if we are to become followers of Jesus.

On the Shoulders of Others

As I've said, most of my early shaping as a follower of Jesus came from my dad and his ministry as my pastor. As a young man in his church, I sensed a call to be a pastor. At the end of each service, it was our tradition to invite the congregation to make a decision to receive Jesus as Savior, rededicate one's life, or surrender to Christian ministry via a call to become a pastor.

To accept this call, one Sunday night I walked down the aisle at the end of the service, where I met the pastor, my dad, standing there to receive me. I said to him, "I feel God is calling me to preach." I'm sure my dad saw it coming because he seemed in no way surprised. He said something like, "That's great, Son. Come by my office this week, and I will help you prepare your first sermon." Later that week, I showed up at my dad's office, where he gave me a couple of books on how to preach as well as a date for delivering my first sermon. (You'll note that he is sort of a no-nonsense kind of guy. For him, if God calls you to do something, then you do it.)

Within a few weeks I had preached that first sermon, thanks to the opportunity he had given me, and I became one of about a dozen men in our church who had felt some kind of calling to vocational ministry. I watched my dad invest his life in these men, teaching and training us with every opportunity. Whenever he went to the hospital to visit the sick, he took one of us with him. When he spoke at funerals, one of us was always around. Every Monday, we had breakfast and prayer with a group of his closest pastor peers. During one of these breakfasts, I heard him say to one of his pastor friends, "Jack, aren't you taking a vacation soon? Well, this is my son, David. God has called him to preach, and he's available to fill in for you." Sure enough, a few weeks later, I found myself standing in Jack's pulpit in his absence. As a young preacher under my dad's tutelage, I often found myself standing among unfamiliar congregations in the name of gaining experience.

I didn't realize how unique this was until I went to seminary a few years later, where I met many people who had been called to ministry years before but had yet to preach their first sermons or even to serve in any kind of church. I was then and remain grateful to my dad for all he put into training me, teaching me, and preparing me for a lifetime of ministry. Even after thirty years of his ministry, I am still in awe as he continues to invest in these young pastors, so you might imagine the sense of honor and pride I felt to receive an e-mail that day, pointing out my small part in living the legacy of my father.

Qualifying the Unqualified

As I reflect on the experience of serving in my dad's church, I realize he wasn't only investing in young preachers; he was working to leave a legacy with almost everyone he knew. As a teenager, I experienced quite a bout of rebellion. I was nineteen before I found my way back to Christ and the church, and it wasn't much later that I sensed God's working in my life. Long before I felt the call to vocational ministry, my father encouraged me to serve in a significant way.

Once when a neighboring church had donated an old bus to us, a group of my friends from a Bible study class approached him about starting a ministry of picking up local kids whose parents didn't attend church. I still recall the look on his face of mixed surprise, pleasure, and wariness. He knew this ministry involved a lot of risks. Who would lead it? If we were successful, it would mean dozens of new kids in our church. What would we do with them? He knew it would cost thousands of dollars, so how would we pay for it? Ultimately, he gave us permission and allowed his twenty-year-old son to start this ministry from scratch. It was my first significant ministry, and, with my father's encouragement, the ministry took off.

One of the neatest things that happened during this time was when one of my dad's pastor friends approached him about hiring me to serve as a summer intern in his church. Our churches were less than two miles apart, and the ministry I had started with the donated bus was growing at a rapid pace, with dozens of volunteers involved. True to form, however, my dad wasn't as interested in hanging on to us as he was about sending us out. I'm sure it would have been easy for him to say, "No, he's not ready," to his friend's request, but I'm thankful he was willing to take the risk and let go. He knew that as important as it was for him to invest his time in us and give us opportunities within the church, it was even more important to let us go out into the world.

I imagine that one of the most difficult things Jesus did was let go of His disciples and push them out into the world. Yet He did because He knew they would ultimately accomplish even greater things through the empowerment of the Holy Spirit. I think my dad also knew greater things would be accomplished not only by letting me go but by letting others go as well. Simply put, following Jesus is about letting go; consider the Great Commission: "Go . . ." (Matt. 28:19a).

I've written about the impact my dad has had on my life—I am who I am because he believed in me and invested in my life. He believed God's words found in Ephesians 4:11–13: "It was he who gave some to be apostles, some to be prophets, some to be evangelists, and some to be pastors and teachers, to prepare God's people for works of service, so that the body of Christ may be built up until we all reach unity in the faith and in the knowledge of the Son of God and become mature, attaining to the whole measure of the fullness of Christ." My dad preached this Scripture at my ordination service, designed to send me out as a young pastor. I was twenty-two years old and mostly unqualified, yet he believed in me. I still remember his words at my ordination: "It is not your job to do everything, but it is your job to equip others to do it."

It is our job as followers of Jesus, whether we are in vocational ministry or not, to invest our lives in others. Even though I have such a great example of this from my dad, it has taken me years to figure it out in my own life, but I have made a decision to leave what Jesus left behind—people who live like Him and love like Him. This commitment is a deliberate decision we all must make if we are to be followers of Jesus.

Relationship, Not a Program

The foundational passage of Scripture that introduces what it means to be a follower of Jesus is found in Mark 3:13–15: "Jesus went up into the hills and called to him those he wanted, and they came to him. He appointed twelve—designating them apostles—that they might be with him and that he might send them out to preach and to have authority to drive out demons."

Jesus chose twelve men who would help accomplish His work and in whom He would invest His life. Notice the words, "He appointed twelve—designating them apostles—that they might be with him." This is amazing to me. There was no program, no over-structured process, no book, no curriculum; He simply chose twelve guys and lived life with them. He lived His life in front of them, and they observed Him living and loving. No large organization, merely a natural, simple, organic process of living life together.

This is profound to me! I have always felt the pressure to gather a few people in order to undertake a regimented program. It never occurred to me that Jesus gathered these twelve simply to live life alongside them. Obviously, this is not to say that His life had no structure or purpose to it; it most definitely did. Jesus was filled with purpose. The second part of this passage reminds us of this: "that he might send them out to preach and to have authority to drive out demons." Not only did He call them to hang out with Him, but He called them to accomplish His purposes. A careful examination of the life of Jesus provides clear insight into what it means to leave a legacy. In short, we see that Jesus employed simple practices when it came to qualifying a group of unqualified disciples. In the context of doing real life with these twelve guys, Jesus did four things:

1. *He shared a vision for His kingdom.* The vision of bringing the kingdom of heaven to earth was radically different from the religious world the disciples were accustomed to, so Jesus took every opportunity to explain His vision to the disciples. He spent a lot of time phrasing and rephrasing it, using different explanations and metaphors to make it easier for them to understand.

2. *He modeled a new way of life.* Jesus demonstrated what it meant to live in the context of the kingdom by loving God and loving people. He rarely went at it alone; He often took the entire group of disciples with Him. At other times He focused on the inner circle of Peter, John, and James. Notice in the Gospels that He never missed an opportunity to model the way and to explain His actions to the disciples.

3. *He enabled them to live His way.* Jesus didn't do everything Himself; He modeled the way only to enable His twelve disciples to do likewise. In essence, He qualified the unqualified by showing them they had what it took to bring the kingdom of heaven to earth.

4. *He encouraged them to live His way.* Enabling others can be messy business, and qualifying the unqualified can be difficult. Jesus's disciples often stumbled, as we still do. But after these experiences, Jesus gathered His disciples together and debriefed, all the while encouraging their hearts.

What Jesus did was intentional, but it was also very organic. While we've found that the methods Jesus employed to train His disciples generally fell into these four categories, we also know that Jesus and the disciples didn't follow a program. This serves to help us understand that we, too, can make a difference in others' lives; we can, and must, leave what Jesus left behind.

A Way of Life

In the wake of Jesus's time on earth, we find people so impacted by His life that they could not help but live and love like Him. Peter is a good example. When the religious authorities were trying to get the early followers of Jesus to stop preaching and teaching about Jesus after His death, Peter's response was, "We cannot help speaking about what we have seen and heard" (Acts 4:20).

Leaving what Jesus left behind is much more art than science, and an effective legacy is much more often from the overflow of the heart than from the programming of the brain. It often surprises me that, when I look back on the fruit left in my life by those who have led me, the moments of greatest impact have seldom been planned or programmed. I've learned from these experiences that when you live like Jesus and love like Jesus, you often can't help but bear fruit.

A young pastor recently told me that his life's mission statement was clarified for him by something I challenged him with. The funny thing is, I remember very little of what I said to him. A missionary I know claims that God used something I said to him while he was burned-out on ministry to renew his calling and save his ministry. Ironically, he was the same guy God used to help me understand my calling. Truly, God works in strange ways.

Intentionality

Make no mistake that while leaving a legacy is an art, it still takes intentionality. I've often heard it said that there is no limit to what God can do through you if you don't care who gets the credit. It was this same statement I once heard God whisper in my ear as I sat in my office. It was in protest to the emotions I was experiencing at the time, having felt I had gotten the proverbial short end of the stick in a particular situation. But God wanted to live and love through me. It was right after I surrendered to live like Jesus on this matter that God used me to develop and implement a church-planting training strategy that would eventually raise up church planters throughout North America. Today, thousands of church planters have been trained, and nearly a thousand churches have been planted as a result of this ministry. The cool thing is I don't think many people remember my involvement. I hope they don't.

We really make this thing of leaving a legacy too difficult. When you live as Jesus lived and love as Jesus loved, you are going to leave what Jesus left behind. Sometimes it is very intentional; other times it seems to merely happen. It's like being in the right place at the right time—sometimes you are aware of the impact you are having, and other times you are not. Sometimes it can be done through an intense discipleship program, and other times it happens best over a relaxing cup of coffee. When we get to heaven, I wouldn't be surprised to find out that some convenience store

clerk nobody ever heard of ultimately left one of the greatest lega-
cies in history through small, nameless acts of love and service.
That will be cool.

The important thing is to find your niche for leaving a legacy.
The thing that drew me to where I now serve is the young staff.
I'm now in my late forties, and when I took this position, I saw an
opportunity to invest in a group of guys nearly half my age. What
excites me most is that these guys are going to be around a lot longer
than I am. And they are part of my legacy.

Serving at Mountain Lake affords me the opportunity to serve
in a number of areas that maximize my passions and strengths. One
of my responsibilities is overseeing our World Care emphasis. World
Care is exactly what it sounds like—our ministry to the world. Our
mission as a church is "to allow God to create an atmosphere where
others can belong in a healthy relationship with God and others and
become more like Jesus every day." In short, we want to help people
belong and become, and we believe that we belong and become so
we can have greater impact. Each year we send hundreds of volunteers around the world to one of our World Care partners in New
Orleans, Las Vegas, Jamaica, Egypt, or Malawi.

I try to go as often as I can because I have learned that when
I spend time with people in this kind of context, the opportunity
for life change grows exponentially. It is one of the simple ways
I have found that I can leave what Jesus left behind. I've also learned
that it is not so much where you go but whom you take with you. I
love what a friend once told me: "It's not what hill you take, but it's
whom you take the hill with." Therefore, as often as I can, I identify
two or three people I can pour my life into and challenge them to
identify two or three people they can pour their lives into, and,
exponentially, we go out to care for the world.

Be You

As I reflect on my life, I have come to understand that I am a starter, a catalyst. I have my greatest impact when I am moving from one exciting challenge to the next (perhaps I should be tested for attention deficit disorder). I am one of those guys who gets bored quickly, and thus I don't fit into many of the traditional religious boxes created over the years. At the same time, I know I have had the opportunity to touch a lot of people. I pray that when I'm gone I will have left behind people who live like Jesus and love like Jesus. However, in most cases it is not because I have spent hours and hours immersed in one-on-one relationships or have practiced intense discipleship regimens. Frankly, I'm still trying to figure out how to have a regular quiet time every day (I'm up to about 75 percent of the time). At the same time, I tend to be somewhat of an introvert, so I find myself spending long periods of time listening to God. I feel an amazing closeness to Him daily as I hear His voice in my quietness.

Perhaps this is a tension that many of us live with. For a lot of us, when it comes to leaving what Jesus left behind, our greatest challenge is this kind of religious baggage. When we think of leaving what Jesus left behind, we think of order, programming, regimen, and discipline. Nothing is wrong with these things, but so often they replace the things that matter most—actively loving God and loving people. We fail to see our relationships in a natural, organic way, and so we struggle when it comes to thinking of leaving what Jesus left behind in those terms. We find it challenging to think about our legacy in terms of the types of risks we take when living as He lived and loving as He loved. Jesus chose to live life together rather than assume a particular regimented program. We must choose to spend time with people if we are to make a difference.

Less Is More

I find it incredibly interesting that Jesus limited his most inti-mate experiences and conversations to three guys. It seems to me that this is constantly a challenge because people are always com-peting for our time. Limiting whom we relate to is often seen in a negative light, but at the same time it is clearly what Jesus did.

For me this means investing in three guys more than anyone else. The first is the lead pastor in the church where I now serve. My relationship with him is unique because I began praying for him before I even knew him. At the time I met him, I was praying for God to bring a young pastor into my life who could plant a church in my community. At the time we didn't have a church in our area that was highly missional. After I got to know him, I was convinced he was the right guy to plant a church. I later found out that while I was praying for a pastor, he was a pastor praying for a place, and there is no doubt in my mind that God put us together. For the first few years we met on a regular basis to encourage and pray for one another, and in recent years we have served together at Mountain Lake Church. I did and I still do feel a special call to invest in him, as he does me.

I am also investing in one of our other young pastors. He and his wife recently had their first child, and Tami and I enjoy hang-ing out with them. We talk about kids, relationships, and ministry, along with our challenges and struggles. Tami and I gain as much as they do from these encounters, and probably more. He recently referred to me as his life coach. I like that! I want to make a differ-ence in his life.

The third person I spend a lot of time with is one of the guys in our church who helps lead our World Care ministry as a volunteer. He and I go on mission trips together, talk several times each week, and have done various studies together. We have a special friendship because of a common passion for taking the love of Christ to the world. God has a special plan for his life, and I want to be part of it.

Spending time with these guys means I can't spend time with everyone. Although these are not the only people I invest in, they are the guys I spend most of my time with because I believe it is how God has called me to leave a legacy. And because all three of them are anywhere from eleven to twenty-two years younger than I am, I know that long after I am in heaven, these guys will continue on.

Through Others

One of the greatest challenges in leaving a legacy is letting go. Jesus had to release the disciples into the world in order for them to carry out His message. He once told them that "anyone who has faith in me will do what I have been doing. He will do even greater things than these" (John 14:12a). Even as I write this, I'm letting go. My friendships with the three guys I mentioned change constantly because they all need new relationships in order to go where God wants them to go. Although I'm still involved in their lives and I'm always available to them, our relationships are changing. This is the hardest part of leaving a legacy: letting go and allowing the relationship to change over time is like giving away your baby. It isn't easy.

At the same time, creating new opportunities for leaving a legacy is invigorating. Our church recently launched a church-planting residency ministry, and with it God has given me a new vision of what He wants to do in and through me. Over the next year, I am going to invest in two guys who are serving as residents in this ministry, as one who directs traffic and helps them process their experiences. I really believe in these guys; they each have a vision for planting churches, with a laser focus on reaching people disconnected from Jesus and the church. In addition to their vision, they are equipped with a leadership competency and capacity for doing so. Once they spend time in this work among our ministry team, they will be going out to start new movements around the country.

That's our vision as a church and one I embrace personally as a calling. Over the next fifteen years, I envision working with twenty to thirty other men who will then go out and plant new churches, reach the disconnected people around them, and care for our world by mobilizing thousands of volunteers to, in turn, go out and make a difference. I do this because this is what I see Jesus doing when He was on this earth. This is my legacy.

Living on Purpose

What's your purpose? For years I lived my life wondering what I was supposed to do. I did a lot, but I always felt there had to be more to it. Then I wondered, could it be, as my wife has suggested, that one should simply "bloom where you are planted"?

A few years ago, I sensed it was time for a new chapter in my life. I was serving in one of the largest missions organizations in the world, but I knew it was time to move on. I was invited to join one of my friends in a global ministry, and although I really wanted to do it, my family wasn't crazy about it.

Later, I accepted the invitation to join the ministry team of the church we attended and loved. When I communicated with others what I was doing, some immediately understood and others questioned my choice. But this is what I knew: For the first time in my life, I was filled with purpose. I was no longer having long conversations and spending endless hours thinking about what I was going to do next. I learned that purpose is not about location but about heart. When you decide you are going to live out God's purposes wherever you find yourself, God begins to flood your life with more vision than you can imagine.

Wherever you are in life right now, whether you're content or not, whether you think you're in the right place or not, make the most of it. Learn from it. Wherever you find yourself, you can find an opportunity to leave what Jesus left behind.

God has given me a clear vision for the rest of my life: to discover true freedom in Jesus Christ and to enable others to do likewise. I think I spent the first half of my life discovering true freedom, and now I'm spending most of my time enabling others. I don't want you to think that leaving a legacy is only for those who are called to a vocational ministry. It isn't. Leaving a legacy is for all of us. If you are a parent, recognize and embrace your legacy in that role. If you are a business owner, leave your legacy in that business. If you are a football coach, if you work with people in an office, if you live in a community with other people, or if you have friends, there are the makings for your legacy.

Leaving a legacy is that simple. It's about realizing that God has placed you here for a purpose. It's about seeing the purpose and potential behind every relationship. It's about seeing through a different set of lenses as you view those around you. It's not complicated—it's relationships. Leaving a legacy is about leaving people on the earth who live and love as Jesus did. I'm convinced that leaving a legacy is a mind-set and an issue of the heart. I wish I had understood it earlier, and I pray that you will see clearly how God wants you to invest in relational ways in a few people for the rest of your life.

Something to Think About

1. Would you describe yourself as someone who does everything alone or as someone who invests in others?

2. Name two or three people you are currently investing in or whom you plan to begin investing in.

3. What steps do you need to take today if you are to leave what Jesus left behind?

Book 2

How Do People Become Followers of Jesus?

As a young pastor, I once visited an elderly lady in the hospital. She was sleeping when I arrived, so I stayed out in the hall in an effort not to disturb her. As I backed out of the room and turned around, I noticed a gentleman in the room directly across the hall. It seemed as if he were inviting me in with his eyes. I stepped into his room and introduced myself as a pastor. He was friendly and eager to talk. Within a few moments I asked him whether he was a Christian. His response almost shocked me. He said, "No, I'm not, but I sure ought to be." I responded by explaining my belief that many people weren't Christians because they simply didn't know how to become one. He agreed, and I went on to ask his permission to tell him how he could become a follower of Jesus. In less than ten minutes, I was able to tell him that God loved him and created him for a very special purpose; that sin had entered the world and separated him from that love and purpose; that Christ died for his sin so that he could be reunited with God; and that by inviting Jesus into his life and asking for His forgiveness, he could know God and God's purpose for his life. I offered to lead him in a prayer inviting Jesus into his life, and he agreed. We celebrated his new life that day, but after I left the hospital room a short time later, I never saw him again.

I believe in divine encounters—I had one that day. However, lately I've noticed that my divine encounters look different. One example is with my friend who hadn't been to church in thirty years and is now attending, trying to figure out how God fits into his life. I can see him changing. When he first came to church, he was angry at God for something very painful that happened years ago. Recently when I saw him, I was taken aback by the happiness he seemed to express. He is definitely experiencing life change, but even after nearly a year he is not where my friend was that day in the hospital. He has had numerous conversations with people about what it means to follow Jesus. In many ways he has already started following Jesus. He is praying, serving, giving, attending our church, and participating in a small group, but he still hasn't crossed that line of faith. He is having a divine encounter, but it is much more like a journey than an event. He is searching, believing, belonging, becoming, and going all at the same time. I pray that he will soon cross that line of faith and invite Jesus to be his forgiver and the leader of his life. He is going to become a follower of Jesus—I know it. I've seen it hundreds of times. When he does, we will have the excitement of celebrating this part of his journey with him through baptism.

I tell both of these stories to illustrate that our world has really changed in my lifetime. The first story is about a world in which those who were disconnected from Jesus and the church lived in the same neighborhood with the church. Today, people who are disconnected live in a different world when it relates to Jesus and the church. When churches that are filled with followers of Jesus recognize this, they can make a huge impact when it comes to their mission to go and make disciples.

It is my hope that this realization will help followers of Jesus engage the world with the gospel by understanding the journeys, struggles, and challenges people go through on their way to find Jesus. My friend Bob Roberts has been referring to the church as a missionary for years. Bob has a heart for the world and has done much to mobilize his entire church around this idea of engaging the world. In doing so, he and his church are making an incredible difference.

This part of the book explores what happens when the church sees itself as a missionary and the missionary sees its own community as its mission field. Many churches are discovering this in the contexts in which they serve, and they are seeing a powerful combination. God is doing an amazing work in our world. In *Breaking the Missional Code*, Ed Stetzer and I asked this question: Why do some churches explode while others don't? Those that are exploding understand the new rules of engagement and have allowed God to shape their hearts and their ministries for missional impact. It is my prayer that followers of Jesus and the churches they attend and serve will experience the blessing of this kind of impact.

"So I say to you: Ask and it will be given to you;
seek and you will find; knock and the door will be opened to you."
—LUKE 11:9

CHAPTER 4

Searching: The Pathway to the Soul

In many ways, my friend Wayne represents the world as it is today. Wayne was my next-door neighbor at a time when I was in the experimental stage of being missional in a local setting. I was planting a church at that time, and one Sunday Wayne showed up at church. I taught that morning from John 14:6, in which Jesus said, "I am the way and the truth and the life. No one comes to the Father except through me." It was the concluding lesson of a series designed to move people toward a commitment to Jesus as the one and only way.

I knew Wayne was searching in a big way, so I was encouraged when he told me that my message "got into the trapdoor of his soul," as he put it. For several weeks we met every afternoon for coffee. We talked about faith, life, family, and all the other things true friends discuss. One Monday morning, he showed up at my door. "Can we do lunch today?" Over lunch we talked about the weekend's message, and I saw a clear opportunity to present the gospel. Wayne listened intently, and as we arrived back at my office, I knew he was at the point of an important decision. He looked at me and asked a question I will never forget: "David, would it be OK if I believed in God but not Jesus?"

I wanted to cry out, "No! Haven't you listened to anything I've said? Could I have explained it any more clearly?" But something stopped me. Or rather, someone—I'm certain it was God. I said, "Wayne, this is a great place to begin but not the place I want you to end." We went into my office and continued our conversation. I challenged Wayne, if he believed in God, to ask God to reveal Jesus to him, if Jesus was indeed the one and only way. Wayne agreed. Before Wayne left that day, I prayed for him a very simple prayer: God, Wayne believes in You but is struggling to believe in Jesus. Reveal Jesus to him through the people he meets, the circumstances he finds himself in, the books he reads, and the things he encounters. Amen.

Following this encounter, Wayne and I continued to meet for coffee almost daily. We brought much value to each other's life. Some days we talked about faith or about the weekend's lesson. Our conversations often focused on the experiences Wayne was having as God continued to reveal Himself. Other days, we talked about running a business or about basketball. But all the while, God was faithful to my prayer.

One Sunday following our worship service, Wayne informed me that he and his wife were going to be gone for a few days. They were going on a personal retreat to the mountains to process the things going on in their lives, and he told me he would be in touch when they returned.

Later that week, Wayne came to my front door, like the first time we met. This time, under that same door frame, his voice caught as he said, "Hey, man, I want you to be the first to know that while we were away, my wife and I committed our lives to Jesus as the one and only way." Wayne and his wife spent the weekend processing the many things that had been going on in their lives spiritually, and at the end of that time they decided to follow Jesus. Amen!

The Bible tells us, "He [God] has made everything beautiful in its time. He has also set eternity in the hearts of men; yet they cannot fathom what God has done from beginning to end" (Eccles. 3:11). Wayne was stuck in a struggle to discover his destiny and to uncover meaning in his world. Through a relationship of love, acceptance, and trust, he found a person and place where he could explore a new kind of relationship with God through Jesus. Wayne is like many of the people I encounter who are searching for destiny, meaning, and acceptance.

Destiny

Perhaps Augustine's words, as well as any, explain why men like Peter, Andrew, and Matthew were so eager to follow Jesus that they left everything at a simple beckoning. Augustine put it this way: "My heart is restless until it finds its rest in Thee." There is something restless about humankind.

A while back, I had dinner with a gentleman who was searching. I was with a friend who asked him about his spiritual background. Though in his fifties, this man told us that he had never had any kind of spiritual background until the past year when he started attending the church where both of us serve. (Sadly, this is not unusual in our world today.) He went on to say something like, "I have homes, cars, boats, and planes, but nothing has done for me what the past year has done in terms of fulfillment." He explained that he didn't fully believe yet, but he was on the way to finding what he was searching for. A few weeks later he invited Jesus into his life and was baptized.

I can certainly relate to his search, and I'm sure you can as well. We all long for this sense of destiny. By destiny I mean we all sense the need to be connected to some kind of larger purpose. We long to know our lives count for something bigger and more significant than our own little world. Even as followers of Jesus, we can lose our way as it relates to our destiny, and I think this is especially true if we have been at it for a long time. My wife recently talked to someone who, after years of living a life of purpose, is struggling to figure out what is next.

Of late, I believe that I have found the sweet spot of my destiny. I can't explain it, but after years of following Jesus, I feel I've hit a new gear as His purpose for my life has become clearer. It's not that I have arrived. It's not that I don't have occasional moments in which I still want to look for greener pastures. There are still times that I find myself asking, "Is this it?" I believe all of this is how God has wired us; otherwise, we would quickly grow complacent and bored.

Paul understood this search. In spite of his success as a Pharisee, he left all to follow Jesus. In Jesus he found what he was looking for, yet at the same time he still had a certain discontent. Listen to what he had to say: "Brothers, I do not consider myself yet to have taken hold of it. But one thing I do: Forgetting what is behind and straining toward what is ahead, I press on toward the goal to win the prize for which God has called me heavenward in Christ Jesus" (Phil. 3:13–14).

My search for destiny required rethinking the way I was living my life. I used to believe my life was on a good path and saw no reason to deviate from it. I soon realized, however, that I was on a broad path, the dangerous kind that Jesus described in the Sermon on the Mount (Matt. 7:13). My path narrowed as I received an invitation to join the team of a young church plant in my community. I was immediately aware that this invitation involved two things: risk and surrender. It seemed to be the kind of decision that people whisper about when you walk by; it didn't make sense. It required a significant pay cut and sacrificing the national platform I held in my current role. It meant moving into a position behind the scenes and relating to a staff only slightly older than my children. While some thought I had lost my mind, it invigorated me. I realized it was the first decision I had made in years that required intentional surrender.

It is in this role that I have found my destiny. I know why I was created, and I know what I'm going to be doing the rest of my life. For the first time in years, I have attained an odd kind of contentment that resulted from my discontent. And all of this took place because I discovered a freedom in Jesus that allowed me to choose to become more like Jesus in my decisions. I didn't have to; I really wanted to, and that has made all the difference.

Please know that I am no different from the rest of humankind—each of us was created with a longing to achieve our destiny, to understand why we exist. We long for a sense of adventure and purpose. Frankly, I think this is why books like *The Purpose Driven Life* have been widely embraced by the general population, not only by followers of Jesus. God has created us for His purposes, and until we connect those dots and find that purpose, we will continue to search. A common mistake we make is to assume that once we find Jesus, the search ceases, but what really happens is that the search finds a new context. It never really ends.

As we consider this search for destiny, it provides the framework for understanding people who are disconnected from Jesus and the church. It explains why even though we may achieve significant success, something seems to be missing. Over and over again I have seen people arrive at a certain point in their lives, simply to say, "Is this it?" Yet Jesus comes into our ordinary existence and gives it purpose. What we discover along the way is that our destiny is a person, not a place. His name is Jesus.

Meaning

When you have two children, it is sometimes difficult to believe they both came from the same womb with similar genetic makeup. One of my kids never questions issues related to faith. My other child began asking questions early on. You know the routine. What does that mean? Why are we doing this? Why did that happen? My son's questions always went deep—he seemed to process his circumstances at a profound level. When a tragedy occurred, he always seemed to be deeply touched. When the World Trade Center buildings fell, he seemed to process it on a more heartfelt level than most of us. When he sits down and talks with people, he seems to connect with who they are and what they are feeling in a way I usually cannot. People young and old seek him for counsel. They always leave with a feeling of connection to him.

In many ways my son is no different from the rest of us. The way we all define meaning is by answering the "why" question, and the collective answers to these questions about life form our worldview. I grew up with a worldview in which there was one God who created the world and all of us in it. I believe that through our deliberate act of disobedience, we are separated from God and from His purpose for our lives. I believe He came into the world in human form, as Jesus, to die for mankind in order to reconcile us to Himself. I believe He left us here and filled us with His Spirit to continue His redeeming work. And I believe that one day He will come again and make all things new. That's my worldview. It comes directly from Scripture, and it supplies meaning and purpose for my life, whether my questions are about suffering, joy, life, or death.

When I became a follower of Jesus as a young teenager, the distance from my head to my heart was very short. Today our world has shifted. The road to meaning is littered with many different ideologies and worldviews. Today's young people are as likely to have a Hindu worldview as they are a Christian one. However, at the same time, they are more likely to have a blending of worldviews rather than one or the other, largely because of the blending of cultures. And in America, this is especially true as our country becomes more and more the ethnic melting pot of the world.

This search for meaning is an invitation to open and honest dialogue for those who are searching and trying to make sense of this seemingly senseless world. Jesus came teaching that the kingdom of God was at hand. On occasion my kids responded to me with a "whatever" when they didn't want to deal with something. I've found I have a way of doing the same thing. However, Jesus introduced us to a new reality. No longer is "whatever" appropriate. He reminds us that there is a new kingdom in play, and that more is going on than meets the eye. He calls us to rethink our world in the context of His spiritual kingdom and to view the world in a whole new way.

Acceptance

To me, the childhood playground is one of the most striking images of acceptance. At the start of any sandlot baseball game, there comes the requisite choosing of teams, and often the most popular or the most talented is given the godlike responsibility of choosing the team. I was never the athlete, so I was often chosen toward the end of the "draft." I hated this experience, but as I grew up and matured, I began to be chosen earlier, and sometimes I even got to do the choosing. Even as an adult, the feeling of being chosen in the early rounds—of being accepted as a desirable team member—launches my self-worth sky high.

I believe this explains a lot of our behavior when it comes to searching. We are desperate for acceptance. When our search is uninformed, it takes all kinds of shapes and forms because people will do nearly anything for acceptance. I often wonder why the disciples so eagerly left everything they had in order to follow Jesus, especially Matthew. Yet acceptance, probably even more than destiny and meaning, drove them. I can sense the isolation Matthew must have experienced as a tax collector. Sure he had friends, but I imagine it was a sort of pseudocommunity, a result of Matthew's power, wealth, and fame. On the inside, Matthew probably felt very alone and wanted to be accepted more than anything else.

The search for acceptance shows up everywhere and explains

much of our behavior. It explains why our teenagers choose sex, regardless of the risks, and why gangs are growing throughout our urban and now suburban areas. It explains why terrorists strap bombs onto their chests and blow themselves up and why some people enter public areas brandishing guns and murdering indiscriminately.

In spite of all of this, and perhaps in foreknowledge of it, Jesus gave us the second-greatest commandment: "Love your neighbor as yourself" (Matt. 22:39). As followers of Christ, often we can easily for lose our way in this area of loving others. It's not that we don't love people but that we don't love people with our actions. I'm often reminded that there is a hurt within every person; there is always more than meets the eye. When I approach people with this in mind, I realize many people simply need to be accepted. My daughter once told me that one of the things she loved about me was that no matter what she did, I still loved her. That is acceptance. We all long for it, and we are created to give it.

The soul's search for destiny, meaning, and acceptance is risky and sensitive. Like sheep that will follow anyone's voice, those who are searching are often led astray. At other times they begin a search that ends prematurely with no resolution. We must keep in mind that caring for a person's soul is our greatest responsibility, for the soul is fragile and has to be handled with care.

It's about the Person

I was sitting in a restaurant in Park City, Utah, several years ago with a group of ministry leaders. Our waitress was a young lady who I later found out practiced witchcraft. One of the guys began a conversation with her in which he began laying out the four spiritual laws: (1) God loves you and has a plan for your life; (2) man is sinful and separated from God; (3) Jesus Christ is God's only provision for man's sin; and (4) we must individually receive Jesus Christ into our lives.

It became apparent she was very uncomfortable with being our waitress, and as a matter of fact, I tip my hat to her for coming back and even taking our order. If I had been she, I don't think I would have returned to that table only to be accosted about a religion I didn't know anything about, from five guys who had advanced degrees on the subject.

The first thing we noticed when she came back was where she stood. She had moved to the side of the table opposite where she stood earlier and was now next to me and my associate from California. The two of us tried to ease the tension by talking to her about herself. She began to tell us how she was part of a small group that met in a home and practiced white magic, which I found incredibly interesting. I told her I was also part of a small group that met in a home, and we studied the teachings of Jesus. I asked her if she had ever heard of Jesus, and she hadn't. To my amazement she seemed completely at ease with our conversation. I encouraged her to check out Jesus through a group of writings called the Gospels, and she genuinely seemed interested.

I believe that if I had lived in Park City this could have been the beginning of a friendship and an ongoing dialogue, but that was the only time I've seen or talked to that young lady. But here is what I know to be true: God is sovereign, and He loves and cares for that young lady far more than I do. He is capable of bringing people into her life who will live like Jesus, love like Jesus, and leave what Jesus left behind, which in this case is a young lady whose search could ultimately lead her to a life that follows Christ.

Living and Loving

Imagine for a moment a vast sea of people committed to simply living like Jesus and loving like Jesus among those who have yet to come to know Him. What if someone in Park City got to know that young lady and simply loved her as Jesus would? What would that look like? It could revolutionize the world. Those who are searching need, more than anything, people and places committed to living and loving like Jesus.

On the whole, my experience has been that people are genuinely open to talking about Jesus and exploring His teachings. However, when I talk about the church, defenses go up, and often conversations cease. This is a dilemma. People who begin their search far away from Jesus need time to explore and a place to experience Jesus, and I'm still convinced that this place is the church. Yet the church is often a barrier when it comes to this search, a barrier often related to the church's image and culture. We have all heard it said, "The church is filled with hypocrites," or "Those people are weird." My daughter was recently telling me about a comment one young atheist made to her that "religion is for the weak." This presents a challenge for us who are followers of Jesus and for our churches.

But what if the church became the missionary and we saw our communities as the mission fields?

Being the missionary right here requires going missional as a church by going into our communities and living and loving like Jesus. However, it doesn't stop there—it can't stop there. We also go missional when we bring those outside the church back with us to meet the rest of the family. We go missional every weekend by taking those barriers seriously and doing everything in our power to remove them. We approach our weekends as missionaries, as if we are on foreign soil, having church with a group of people who do not understand our language or strange culture. In our book *Breaking the Missional Code,* Ed Stetzer and I talked about the need to give up our preferences: "Simply put, being missional does not mean doing things the way we like them. It means taking the gospel into the context where we have been called . . . and to some degree, to let the church take the best shape it can in order to reach a specific culture. However, the problem is our preferences. You can't be missional and pick what you like at the same time."[1]

Giving up our preferences can be a challenging thing. It means developing an authentic faith community that puts the preferences of lost and disconnected people before our own. And not only does it mean giving up our preferences as it relates to our faith community, but it also means giving up our preferences as it relates to our lives.

While every community and context will have its own set of cultural barriers, there are overarching themes when it comes to being the church in your mission field: relevance, authenticity, and trust.

Relevance

Those who are searching are looking for a grander purpose (destiny), trying to make sense out of an event or crisis (meaning), or are experiencing isolation and loneliness (acceptance). When we address the needs related to their searches, we become relevant. Being relevant is about meeting people where they are, right in the middle of their needs. If I am hungry and you feed me, you are relevant. If I am lonely and you visit me, you are relevant. If I am sick and you heal me, you are relevant. If I am in grief and you comfort me, you are relevant. If my marriage is hopeless and you give me hope, you are relevant. Living and loving like Jesus will make us relevant.

Authenticity

So often I think those who are disconnected from Jesus and the church do not see followers of Jesus as real people. We become the barrier. They often express what they see with words like *hypocrite*. They know we are not perfect; they see our mistakes and blemishes. They also wish we could see them. Being real about who we are and where we are has a way of neutralizing the playing field. One of the big turning points in my relationship with my neighbor, Wayne, was when he began to bombard me with a lot of really difficult questions, and I simply replied, "I don't know." He was incredulous. "What do you mean you don't know?" I told him, "I don't know, but my not knowing doesn't affect my trust in God."

Why do we, as followers of Jesus, think we have to have all the answers? I believe this is the difference between having a relationship with Jesus and practicing a religion. If you are interested in religion, you need all the answers. If you are interested in following Jesus, you don't have to have all the answers because you can trust Him.

I spoke with a lady in my small group who is facing a great disappointment in her life. She expressed how she had vented to God and how she had even been angry with Him. I told her I thought God wanted her to be honest with Him, that I thought He could handle her disappointments. I could see the look of relief and hope come over her.

Trust

I believe those I know, I can trust, and I trust those who are honest and those I know truly care for me. I trust those who have a track record of trust. It is important to be relevant and authentic because it leads to trust. When people who are disconnected from Jesus see us truly living like Jesus and loving like Jesus, the chances are that this witness of our lives will cultivate trust in them. As it has been said, "Preach the gospel at all times. If necessary, use words."

A Beautiful Bride

Imagine for a moment a faith community committed to relevance, authenticity, and trust. Imagine a place where no matter how deviant the sinner, you know you can bring your lost friends and family and they will be accepted. Imagine a place where you know that the deepest needs of your coworker will be spoken to. Imagine a place of faith, hope, and love, a community of faith so compelled by the issues and challenges of our culture that the members of that community are actively engaged in acts of kindness, mercy, and social justice.

When people come to grasp what it means to be a follower of Jesus, this is exactly what happens—the church becomes a place for the soul. The apostle Paul understood this and painted, to me, one of the most beautiful and evocative pictures of the church: "Husbands, love your wives, just as Christ loved the church and gave himself up for her to make her holy, cleansing her by the washing with water through the word, and to present her to himself as a radiant church without stain or wrinkle or any other blemish, but holy and blameless" (Eph. 5:25–27).

Have you ever seen an ugly bride? I doubt it. There is something about the moment at the beginning of a wedding when the processional march begins and we stand and turn our heads toward the bride. We are caught up in the moment as she, with her father, makes her way to the altar, where she will be given away in a grand gesture.

This a picture of the church arrayed in all of her splendor. This is also a picture of what can happen every weekend when we come together. This is her moment. Let the marriage feast begin.

Something to Think About

1. What does it mean for the church to be the missionary in your context?

2. Describe how you can best help those who are searching for the way of Jesus.

3. Describe how you can partner with other followers of Jesus in your church to assist those on the journey.

"I am the way and the truth and the life.
No one comes to the Father except through me."
—JOHN 14:6

CHAPTER 5

Believing: Jesus Is the Way

I recently witnessed one of the most powerful and moving experiences of my life—203 people spontaneously going public with their faith in our weekend services. Not only did I witness it, but I got to participate by baptizing half of them. The next day, my arms were sore. It was awesome!

Our ministry team had the idea for a message series called "H$_2$O." We had been praying and planning for weeks, but to be honest, we had no idea how God would use this series to galvanize the faith of so many people. I don't believe that any of us thought so many people would respond and come to be baptized. It was truly one of those "immeasurably more than all we ask or imagine" moments that Paul talked about (Eph. 3:20a). The amazing thing is that it happened again the next weekend, when another 143 people went public with their faith and were baptized. Over two weekends we saw 346 people demonstrate their belief through baptism.

Many scholars suggest that we are experiencing a third spiritual awakening today. I think it is true—all indications are that people are more spiritually aware than ever before. However, and this is a crucial distinction, that is not to say that they are awakening to Jesus. This movement is global, but it is not identified with any one faith. Some people are turning to a new form of spirituality, while others are embracing older forms of religion. No longer are we living in a simple world in which some people become Hindu and others become Christian. Today, many are choosing a little of this and a little of that, blending a new kind of spirituality. It's true that many circles are embracing Jesus, but they are embracing Him as *a* way rather than *the* way.

With a Capital *T*

The statement that "Jesus is the way—the only way" often brings a lot of heat. Those of us who believe this are often considered to be narrow in our views and bigoted in our response to other religions. Yet Jesus was very clear when He responded to Thomas's question by saying, "I am the way and the truth and the life. No one comes to the Father except through me" (John 14:6).

In short, Christianity stands unique when it comes to its religious worldview. Other religions are about man's attempt to make his relationship right with God, whereas Christianity is God's attempt to have a relationship with man. In many other religions, man takes the initiative, but in Christianity God is the initiator. Other faiths are attempts to seek God, yet in Christianity Jesus seeks us. In many religions I am made right with God through enlightenment, ritual, achievement, or even arbitrary selection by God. In Christianity, God pursues man, reconciling him to Himself through Jesus. Paul put it this way: "For it is by grace you have been saved, through faith—and this not from yourselves, it is the gift of God—not by works, so that no one can boast" (Eph. 2:8–9).

It seems like an easy choice to those of us who have already committed to following Jesus: why would you subject yourself to physical and mental requirements (or worse yet, random selection) when you could simply accept the grace that God freely offers? In the context of my decision to follow Jesus in the 1970s, this was not an issue. It was Jesus or nothing. For many of us who grew up in the Bible Belt or in Christian homes, the same was true. However, when it comes to spiritual matters, the world has radically changed. Today many who come to be followers of Jesus do so only after overcoming considerable barriers and challenges as they pertain to other faiths they have encountered.

Many of the 346 people baptized on the two weekends represent this challenge. They came from many different religious and faith traditions. Some of their journeys to Jesus were short, while others had to travel a great distance. For some their greatest challenge was embracing Jesus as the one and only way, and for others this was easy. Many of them had been attending our church on the weekends, participating in volunteerism and small groups for months or years, and others had come only recently.

Becoming a missional follower of Jesus involves helping those who are searching to navigate the terrain as they move toward the belief that Jesus is indeed the only way. Gaining insight into the journey of those searching can greatly benefit us in helping those who are moving toward belief. Being a missional follower of Jesus is about getting outside ourselves and into their world, their lives, their minds, and their search.

Believing Requires Time

I remember the first time I heard someone talk about becoming a follower of Jesus in terms of worldview conversion. The lightbulb came on for me. All of a sudden it made sense that believing requires much time for many people. The speaker explained that when a person—consciously or subconsciously—begins a search for faith, he or she is essentially trying to find some sense in life, and the way a person typically does this is through development or adoption of a worldview. This worldview is a lens through which we see and understand the world: why we exist, why we suffer, why we die, why we struggle with evil, and why we live, for a few examples. All of a sudden I understood why it took so long for some people to come to Jesus.

I can only imagine the time it takes to rethink all these ideologies. I realized that more often than not, when someone becomes a follower of Jesus, it requires a total reorienting of life. When I became a follower of Jesus, it was much easier because I had grown up in a churched environment, hearing stories about Jesus. I never questioned who Jesus was, and I didn't have to give up any other beliefs. I simply made a commitment to do what I already knew was right.

Worldviews are complicated. They are forged over time and personal experience, and the likelihood is that one hundred different people will have many different worldviews. It is important to note here that bringing a person to acceptance of Jesus as the way does not mean converting that person to a worldview; it means giving that person a new lens—which is the grace of God—through which to examine his or her existing worldview. For a man who comes to accept Jesus following years of addiction, there are years of recovery ahead of him as he replaces the crutch of substance abuse with the buttresses of Jesus. The same is true for someone coming from a different religious worldview. It often takes years for Jesus to clean out the house of competing ideologies and behaviors.

Maybe our churches need to be more like twelve-step programs for those in spiritual recovery. We need to recognize that, the majority of the time, conversion is not the immediate result of a miraculous revelation. As I said earlier, searchers require relevance, authenticity, and trust in their investigations of Christ, and this process continues into the journey of belief.

Believing Requires a Safe Place

Consider the vocational missionary: She travels to people who are far from God and translates the gospel into a language they can understand and relate to. If those assertions are true and it takes time for people to change the lens through which they see the world, then there has to be a context in which people can work through these issues and barriers. Perhaps this is why God established the church. Examine with me the Acts church: "Each one heard them speaking in his own language. Utterly amazed, they asked: 'Are not all these men who are speaking Galileans? Then how is it that each of us hears them in his own native language?'" (Acts 2:6b–8). Maybe what God had in mind was a community of grace and love to which people who did not know Him could come and be honest about their struggles in a comfortable, relevant environment.

Jim attended our church every weekend for several months, but his consistent habit of arriving just in time to hear the message and leaving before the closing prayer made it clear to me that he was there in a search for answers. As we built a friendship, I learned that Jim grew up in a home of competing ideologies; his father was an avowed atheist, while his brother was a Scientologist. Understandably, Jim wasn't sure what he believed. He was open to exploring the claims of Christ, and he chose our church as a safe place to explore those claims. Over time Jim became a follower of Jesus, but in the meantime he needed a safe place to have his questions answered and time to process the answers.

Exploration in a safe place is often the searcher's initial step to believing, but participation is a crucial next step in this progression. As is clear from Jim's story, many are not willing to commit to following Jesus without first looking under the hood, so to speak. When I made the decision a few years ago to trade in my sports car for a pickup truck (which is culturally relevant here in north Georgia), I spent months researching makes and models, crash-test safety ratings, and towing capacity. I added, subtracted, multiplied, and divided until I had come to the price I was willing to pay. I spent weeks researching and processing the issues relevant to purchasing a truck. I even test-drove a few competitive versions before I finally made a decision. I did all this for a vehicle that I will drive for, at most, ten years.

Certainly, my intent here is not to cheapen the decision to become a follower of Jesus by comparing it to purchasing a means of transportation, but I think you will agree that looking under the hood is a responsible aspect of making a big decision. When it comes to issues of faith, it is healthy and necessary for a searcher to examine the faith community, not only in its form but also its function. The problem is that many well-intended Christians expect those who are searching to conform to the ways of the church before they become committed followers of Jesus.

Pardon the analogy, but what if we were insistent that our community of faith be a safe place where people can come and test-drive the faith and look under its hood prior to purchase? What if we allowed those who are disconnected from Jesus to be involved with the church in every way? What if we encouraged those who are disconnected to serve beside connected believers in significant areas of volunteerism? What if we encouraged those who are disconnected to experiment with greater impact by going into other cultures to make a tangible difference? What if devoted followers of Jesus invited those who are searching not only into our church building but into our homes for meaningful community? Is this not the way of Jesus? Not only did He sit and eat in the homes of sinners, but He also invited His disciples into a relationship with Him prior to their understanding of Him as the way.

Believing Requires Relationships

I was a middle school student-manager for the high school track team when I accompanied the team to a meet at the University of South Carolina. Also participating in the meet was the (then) Baptist College. I remember thinking how odd it was that the school had the words *Baptist College* plastered across its jerseys (evidently, the school realized it, too, and later changed its name). As a kid who knew very little about Christianity, I remember thinking that they were weird; this unchurched kid found the word *Baptist* intimidating. Today, this memory causes me to ponder how those who are disconnected from Jesus and church feel. I think most of us forget what it was like to be lost and what it takes to help us find the way.

It wasn't until I began planting churches that I realized it was the responsibility of the church and its members to care for the soul, not merely keep it out of hell. I discovered that by creating a safe place for people to come and enter into relationships through which to explore and experience Jesus, many would find Jesus for themselves. To me, this explains why Jesus became a friend to sinners, and so must we.

Tell the Truth

It may seem obvious, but the most important step for those searching is coming to understand the truth of the gospel. Paul understood this when he challenged the church, "How, then, can they call on the one they have not believed in? And how can they believe in the one of whom they have not heard? And how can they hear without someone preaching to them? And how can they preach unless they are sent? . . . Consequently, faith comes from hearing the message, and the message is heard through the word of Christ" (Rom. 10:14–15a, 17).

In one of my early church plants, I hired an assistant who was not a follower of Jesus. She was a good person but felt no need to bring Jesus into her life. I hired her because I thought it made sense to put our mission for reaching unchurched people into action. I explained to her that one reason I was offering her the job was that she did not attend our church, and she proved to be an excellent employee. One of her responsibilities was to type a handwritten manuscript of my sermon every week, and almost every week she would come in my office and begin a conversation with, "I have a couple of questions about your sermon." We would spend a few minutes talking about the truth within the message, and she would move on. One day she asked if it would be OK for her to visit our weekend services. I assented, and after several months she came into my office and said, "I guess I will have to quit my job if I get baptized and join the church, huh?" She went on to talk about how she had come to believe in Jesus as the way and had decided to follow Him. Of course I celebrated the moment with her and told her I thought we could bend the rules in this case.

There is something powerful about the truth of God's Word. I've discovered, too, that faith comes by hearing, hearing the Word of God. Teaching biblical truth in the context of one's search for destiny, meaning, and acceptance is key to crossing over the line of faith. We can offer safe environments and fulfilling relationships for years, but without the presentation of the truth of the gospel our efforts will be meaningless. On the other hand, if we are honest, teaching platforms in our churches often become platforms for addressing our own preferences. They become more about what to do and what not to do than about Jesus.

When the church provides a safe place among safe people, for those searching to hear the truth of the gospel, they will listen. And when they listen, I believe the power of the gospel and the Holy Spirit will be true catalysts to bringing them to belief. As I reflect on the incredible celebration of watching 346 people make commitments to Jesus and the stories of those commitments, I find that a significant majority of those baptized were people who had been attending our church for years. They had been raised with little or no understanding of Jesus and the church, yet it was their experience in our faith community that drew them to the decision to follow Jesus. Don't underestimate this power.

Something to Think About

1. What does it mean to be a safe place for people to search?

2. Make a list of things your church could do to become a safer place.

3. How can you connect relationally with people who are searching?

4. Make a list of specific people you are going to invest in over time.

5. Describe how you can help them come to grips with the truth.

> *"Love your neighbor as you love yourself."*
> —MATTHEW 22:39

CHAPTER 6

Belonging: Why Can't Church Be More Like . . . ?

Why can't church be more like a family reunion? Why can't church be more like a skate park or a parking lot on Friday night? Why can't church be more like a city park or an English pub? All these and many more are places where we gather and experience community, where we belong in healthy relationships with one another.

A couple of years ago, our church did a message series titled "Why Can't Church Be More like Starbucks?" The focus of the series was to move people toward community, and we had an amazing response. Some people related to the analogy and loved it because they could see the comparison between church and Starbucks. Other people were highly offended, like the lady who sent us this note: "Mountain Lake, serving coffee is one thing, but to advertise an expensive brand as a reason for attending, your congregation if it professes to be Christian (or does it?) is unbelievable. I attend a church that provides worship, spiritual growth and fine music as its goal as well as fellowship if one desires it. . . . Please don't send me any more of your disgusting advertisements." I think it is safe to say she didn't get the premise of the series. The challenge, when it comes to belonging, is that many other people don't get it as well.

It is this kind of response to community that frankly disturbs me. At the same time, if I sat down and talked to anyone who found our series or any of my other questions in the opening paragraph offensive, I don't think we would disagree. We are created for community. We need community. Think of the Garden of Eden, where the need for belonging was woven into the very fabric of Creation. God created the first man after musing, "Let us make man in our image" (Gen. 1:26a), referring to God's communion with His Son and the Holy Spirit. God went on to pronounce that "it is not good for the man to be alone" (Gen. 2:18a), and He subsequently created a woman from the flesh of man. The first and most tragic display of community shattered came as a selfish choice was made, and the man and woman were separated from God as a result of their sinful choice.

The need for community didn't end there, as the value of belonging was clearly played out in the Gospels. Jesus was often surrounded by large crowds of people, thousands at times; yet He chose twelve disciples to be His closest friends. Of the twelve, there were three with whom He shared His most intimate self.

We were created with the need for belonging, and if the church is to be relevant, the first need we should meet is this need for community. I would even venture to go a step further and say it is impossible for us to be the church God had in mind if we do not offer authentic, loving, warm environments where people can belong in healthy community. Being a missional follower of Jesus means offering the disconnected a place to belong, understanding that belonging can be a significant step toward believing.

Intentional Community

Authentic community and belonging are not something we can assume will simply happen. Merely because we attend church regularly or participate in a Bible study group does not mean that we are experiencing belonging at the level that Jesus invites us into. Granted, some days I stumble into community and experience belonging almost by accident; and when it happens, it is really, really good. You know the feeling—that overwhelming sense of relief that comes from hearing, "Me too!" when you've shared a part of yourself with another.

But many people might say that I experience belonging at a different level than most, being a church pastor. Admittedly, I serve on a great team in a great church, and the people I serve with are my best friends. Belonging is the core of our church's mission, and we have one of the best small-group systems in the country with nearly 80 percent of our adult attendees participating in small groups. Yet I can't help but believe there is more.

At the risk of hyperbole, the need for belonging is what got me started on the journey I am on now. When my wife, Tami, was hit by a van, I began a serious assessment of our relationships. I soon discovered that while we had our families, they lived in other states, and no matter how close the relationships seemed, we were hindered by time and space. While Tami was in the hospital recovering, I was astounded by the number of people all over the country who were praying for us, e-mailing, and calling. I loved those people for loving us so much, some of whom I didn't know. Two of our pastors were there that night, yet something was missing. Even with hundreds of people pouring prayers and blessings on us, I knew that authentic, personal relationships were conspicuously absent. We had to admit that we weren't belonging.

Not long after the accident, I was having coffee with my pastor when he asked me about the people at our church who had connected with and cared for us while Tami was recovering. I ran through the list of people who had responded: a couple of pastors, one of the wives, and another couple in the church. I immediately saw the disappointment on his face, but I stopped him and explained that we had no one to blame for this lack of belonging other than ourselves because we had not connected with people in our community or the church. I had traveled all over the country telling people how to create communities in their churches, but I had only attended our church on those occasional times when I was in town, and as a result, Tami and I were dying for belonging.

During that time, I decided to change gears and move my ministry to the local church. I kept having these thoughts that if I died no one would be around to care for my family. I was longing to belong in relationships with others at a more intimate and authentic level. I wanted to love and be loved by close friends and to be in significant, meaningful relationships with people who really knew me at more than a surface level. It was a tall order, though, and I knew it was going to require radical shifts in my life.

Chances are, if you are reading this book and you do not belong in a community of significant relationships, you feel the same tension. Many of us turn to the church to have this need for belonging met, but sometimes the church is not prepared to be that place. But we can become this place, and in so becoming, the church can begin to take shape as a powerful missional tool. If we are really serious about being the missionary and connecting with people, what better way to do so than to meet them in their search and provide a context for unconditional acceptance? The results are often life changing.

Barriers to Belonging

I believe that churches as a whole are reflections of their individuals. Often our churches reflect our busyness in that we have so much going on there isn't time for community. Maybe something happened to create a barrier, a deep divide within a local church that makes authentic relationships seem impossible. Precisely as we can lose our way as individuals, our churches, too, can lose their way. This is why it is so important that we spend time rethinking church and coming to realize that our churches should be made up of networks of authentic relationships joined together for a common good and a common purpose, to be a reflection of Jesus in every way on this earth. Whatever barriers stand in the way of this purpose must be addressed.

I consider two of the primary barriers to be awareness and acceptance. When it comes to awareness, many don't recognize their need for belonging. I once saw a list that ranked countries in terms of group-ness and individual-ness. Countries in the East like Korea and China were at the top of the list in terms of valuing group-ness as a culture, while the United States was at the very bottom of group-ness and at the very top of individual-ness. Here, in one of the most individualized cultures in the world, we think we don't need anything or anyone because our culture has shaped us to be rugged individuals.

One challenge we face as followers of Jesus is helping others become aware of their need for belonging. While our culture is known for its individualism, we really do need one another. We long for acceptance and community, typically seeking ways to belong. The problem we face is encouraging people to experience something at a deeper level than they are aware exists or are convinced they need. I recall a time in my life when I experienced a deep hurt and said to myself, *I will never let anyone hurt me again.* There is something about how we are wired that often recoils when it comes to our relationships. We seek the protection of our own private world, only to discover it is our own private world that puts us at the greatest risk.

Another significant barrier relates to acceptance, and frankly there are few places in life where we find unconditional acceptance. Even our own families are sometimes conditional. We feel a little like the woman caught in the act of adultery: naked and all alone, with a lot of people staring at us and pointing. We, like her, need someone to say, "I accept you." Before I became a follower of Jesus,

I was offered this kind of acceptance when I met a follower who told me, "You are a special person. God has a plan for your life." His simple words spoke acceptance into my life, and even at that very moment I found myself inching toward Jesus.

Acceptance is the gateway to belonging—without it there is no belonging. When we accept others in love, they inch toward the gospel, which is why it is so important for us to reflect Jesus by opening our arms to others. Living and loving like Jesus means there is no limit to this acceptance; reading through the Gospels will show you that the only people Jesus didn't accept were those who failed to accept others, which most often represented the religiously elite Pharisees. Mark's Gospel provides a detailed scenario in which Jesus demonstrated this kind of love: "People were bringing little children to Jesus to have him touch them, but the disciples rebuked them. When Jesus saw this, he was indignant. He said to them, 'Let the little children come to me, and do not hinder them, for the kingdom of God belongs to such as these. I tell you the truth, anyone who will not receive the kingdom of God like a little child will never enter it.' And he took the children in his arms, put his hands on them and blessed them" (Mark 10:13–16).

On another occasion, Jesus told a story of a great banquet in which many of the invited guests failed to appear. Jesus explained, "The owner of the house became angry and ordered his servant, 'Go out quickly into the streets and alleys of the town and bring in the poor, the crippled, the blind and the lame'" (Luke 14:21). Jesus accepted and loved without condition, as we must if we are to be His followers.

This leads us, however, to an interesting question: Are we to accept those like the woman caught in the very act of adultery? Or perhaps the little children? What about the poor, the crippled, the blind, and the lame? Are we to welcome with open arms those like the thief at the cross? Consider the parable of the Good Samaritan

(Luke 10:25–37) and the question that precedes it: Who is my neighbor? Unconditional acceptance of all people is a defining mark of a missional follower of Jesus, and the practical implementation of this acceptance will often be a pathway to belonging.

Committing to Belong

A commitment to belong in relationships with others is a significant step toward becoming like Jesus. A common misconception about belonging is that we must have it all figured out before we can belong in a community of followers of Jesus. What I am finding more and more to be the pattern, however, is that most people belong before they become, meaning that they are in meaningful community with other followers of Jesus even before they become followers themselves. In saying this, I would even go one step further and say that many people belong before they even believe. Those who are searching do so in the context of relationships—they have to try on what it means to follow Jesus before they fully embrace the truth of the gospel.

During the "H_2O" message series I described earlier, we saw entire small groups baptized all at once, a terrific punctuation to the ability of our church to welcome outsiders experiencing and exploring community even before they had professed to believe in Jesus. Can you imagine a church that would exclude people who were not followers of Jesus? Can you imagine a Jesus who would exclude people? The Jesus I love invited people to come follow Him; to experience Him for themselves; and allowed them, over time, to form their own opinions.

I've approached this subject of belonging mostly from the perspective of those disconnected from Jesus and the church. This is an important perspective for those committed to becoming missional followers of Jesus, but it is not the only perspective. As followers of Jesus, we are to belong in healthy relationships with God and other people—being a follower of Jesus is not about consumption but about authentic relationships in which people are accepted and belong at the deepest level.

I once heard someone say, "When Jesus comes into your life, He is rude in that He brings His entire family." When you become a follower of Jesus, you can't continue living for yourself alone, with no community aside from yourself. As followers of Jesus, we have been born into God's family, and as members of His family, we belong in relationships with others. As I've said over and over again, to love God and love people is to live and love like Jesus. That's the point of the gospel. It's not about what we consume, or what we learn, or how much knowledge we have. It's not about how spiritually involved we are or how closely we follow a moral code of conduct. Living and loving like Jesus is about loving God and loving people and belonging in healthy relationships with both.

Creating Spaces

Perhaps it is easy to assume that if I attend church where there is robust fellowship or am part of a small group or Bible study where there is a healthy exchange of ideas and truth, then I can check "belonging" off my list. But both of these things are means to an end, not the end in themselves. We can have good fellowship and be in a good group and not experience belonging in an authentic way. God wants us to belong in relationships, not simply participate in religious activities with one another.

The local church can create a context in which people can belong together, and it can provide a place where those who are searching can belong while they search. Many church leaders have broken the discipleship code already by rethinking church in terms of relationships. Joseph Myers, in his book *Organic Community,* recognized that church should be a place where people naturally connect. He encouraged the church, "Create environments and spaces

that encourage the patterns of belonging and allow people to connect naturally in all kinds of ways."[2]

With this said, all of our churches can encourage organic community if we understand the importance of connecting people. I used to
think that belonging was the result of a particular structure or model,
and that if you had a certain church model you would have belonging; but this is not true. You can have a network of house churches
and still not cultivate healthy relationships that lead to belonging. On
the other hand, you can be part of a twenty-thousand-member megachurch that experiences a sense of belonging at a very deep and intimate level. I do believe that certain forms and expressions of church
lend themselves more toward facilitating a sense of belonging, but
there is certainly not a formula.

Modeling after Jesus

If you look at the way Jesus belonged with people, you will
note that He interacted with them at different levels. There were
the large crowds He related to, cared about, and led; and at the
same time, there were the twelve He chose to be with more intimately. Even out of that twelve, He was especially close to Peter,
John, and James. Jesus was serious about relationships, but He also
knew that He needed to have different relationships with different people and that those He spent the most time with would be
impacted by Him most significantly. He realized that the smaller
the group, the greater the impact. One thing is for sure—Jesus
didn't live in isolation or limit His relationships to those who saw
eye to eye with Him.

To follow the model of Jesus, we must love all people, but at
the same time we must be in community with a few we can really
belong with. For me this means being a part of a small group in my
local church. Out of that small group, I have two or three people
I go deeper with relationally; and I don't believe we can belong

in healthy relationships with God and others without a group of people we are living life with on a regular basis.

It is through the local church that God has created a safe place where we all can belong in healthy relationships with others. Therefore we must allow God to create an atmosphere where He breathes life into our structures if we are to belong.

A Place to Belong

It is not enough to belong in a healthy relationship with God. The Jesus way leads us into healthy relationships with others. The local church provides the context in which this kind of belonging can take place. At the same time, it is not enough to simply belong in healthy relationships with God and others who are followers of Jesus. We must belong to those who are yet to become followers of Jesus. Some are becoming, while others are yet to start the journey. Missional churches and missional followers understand the importance of these connections. They also understand that these connections happen both inside and outside the local church. Here are a few observations and lessons I've learned along the Jesus way about belonging.

- *Being in a group doesn't mean you are going to belong in healthy relationships with others.* Belonging is not something you can program, and it is certainly not something automatic, merely because you are in group. There are good group experiences that promote belonging. There are bad group experiences that challenge us. Sometimes they can be so challenging that we want to give up on belonging.

   I am the key to belonging. When my heart is committed to belonging, then I can experience belonging at a different level. When we share a commitment for belonging, over time we can experience belonging at a deeper, more intimate level. However, this kind of belonging requires time.

- *When it comes to belonging, the size of the church doesn't matter.* The church I have attended and served in for the past eight years has grown rapidly, and we are now moving beyond two thousand in regular weekend worship attendance. At the same time, the sense of belonging among attendees is growing. What I am learning is that valuing belonging and making a commitment to belong are the first steps, regardless of size. We really do believe we exist to belong. Because we believe this, we are constantly working to ensure that people are connecting not only to God but also to one another.

- *People who really want to belong often need help connecting with others.* When it comes to belonging, many people don't know where to begin. Attending our churches can be socially isolating experiences, so connecting people to one another has to be intentional and carried out in simple steps. One of the most important services we can provide as a church is to help people figure out how to connect with one another. Since belonging is our responsibility, we need to work hard to simplify our church structures and programming to eliminate any competition with belonging.

- *Life change happens most often in the context of belonging.* Loving God and people is really what it is all about. It is certainly how Jesus summed up the entire Law. Belonging sets us up to succeed at this. Providing a place or places where people belong in healthy relationships with God and others sets us up to become. It is the Jesus way. Making a decision to connect with others in some type of small group is the most important decision you can make. When this happens and belonging takes place, an environment of life change is created.

It's Not about Curriculum

When it comes to belonging, a common mistake we make is to build our belonging around a kind of curriculum. I love curriculum. I write books. At the same time, our curriculum is a means to an end, not an end in itself. The churches I experienced early got it right in many ways but at the same time had struggles. While Sunday school was a good concept—people studying the Bible—it wasn't structured for maximum impact. Sunday school as I knew it usually consisted of a small group of people meeting one hour before worship. The challenge to our traditional Sunday school was it became all about curriculum. The teacher would stand in the front behind a lectern and lecture. As kids we were forbidden to speak or ask questions, and we sat in rows of chairs where we had to look at the backs of the heads of the people sitting in front of us.

I can't imagine Jesus teaching a Sunday school class, at least not the one I grew up in. However, I can see Him doing life with a small group of people sitting together and debriefing their lives around a common principle related to His way. Imagine how liberating it would be to talk about loving other people and having a real discussion about how that played out in our lives over the past week. Taking it a step further, imagine actually talking about a struggle to love a certain neighbor. Imagine the group encouraging, giving feedback, praying for one another, and even holding one another accountable.

Our goal is not simply to connect people together, but it is to be connected in order that we might relate to one another in the way God has created us to relate—on a deeper level. No matter the curriculum we study, regardless of whether it's a single verse of Scripture or an ancient book of theology, we cannot forget that our purpose in bringing people into community is to grant them the opportunity to form healthy relationships with God and others.

At the end of the day, if we are not loving God and loving people (the Great Commandment) in a Jesus-like way, we have completely missed the point.

Something to Think About

1. Describe an experience in which you participated in a group but failed to belong. What about a time when you participated in a group and really belonged?

2. Identify the barriers to belonging in your own life and context.

3. Describe how you can invite those who are searching to enter into meaningful communities of belonging with followers of Jesus.

4. Identify two or three people who are disconnected from Christ and the church and whom you can intentionally connect with for the purpose of belonging.

"Come, follow me."
—MATTHEW 4:19a

CHAPTER 7

Becoming: Finding the Jesus Way

*R*ecently I flew with three of my teammates into Chicago, where we spent the extra bucks for a global positioning system (GPS). We all fell in love with her; I mean *it*. I don't know why I was holding out on GPS technology, but I am a true believer now. All we had to do was enter the address we wanted, and we were all but there. Our first challenge for our new GPS friend was downtown Chicago's famous Ditka's Restaurant, and she—or rather it—delivered; complete with maps and a pleasant female voice, GPS led us right up to the door's valet. Amazing!

Over the next few days we keyed in countless addresses with the same result. She never failed. If we ignored her, got distracted, or went our own way, she would correct and recalculate our new directions. Complete with a verbal response, "recalculating directions," she began guiding us through a series of turns that would correct our errors and take us safely to our original destination. Even when we didn't know where we wanted to go, we could look up things like hotels, restaurants, and other landmarks and let our GPS friend lead us there.

Where are you going right now? If you are becoming, you are headed somewhere. But imagine waking up one day and realizing that you have arrived at the wrong destination. Wouldn't you love to have a GPS for your life, so all you would have to do is simply type in your intended destination and follow the directions? Consider this: God has a destiny for our lives and wants to navigate the course, and He even recalculates when we move off course.

In a word, His way for our lives is Jesus. Jesus said Himself, "I am the way and the truth and the life" (John 14:6a). When I use the term *becoming,* I mean that we are becoming like Jesus. Becoming is about living like Jesus, loving like Jesus, and leaving what Jesus left behind, which means He left a legacy of people who lived like Him and loved like Him.

Losing Our Way

No one would argue that we have a tendency to lose our way and can often use help recalculating. The Bible tells us "for all have sinned and fall short of the glory of God" (Rom. 3:23). In other words, we have all set out to hit the target of God's purpose for our lives, but somewhere in the journey we lost our way. We have the best of intentions, but nevertheless we wind up lost. The funny (or-not-so-funny) thing is that many times we don't even know we are lost.

Not only do we lose our way as individuals, but we can often lose our way as a church. There are times when we as the church need to recalculate our direction, and I believe this is exactly what Jesus confronted in the religious systems He encountered. Thus He began His public ministry with the word *repent,* which suggests there was (and still is) a need to rethink and redirect. Like the faithful GPS lady following one of my missteps, we must recalculate directions.

Surrender

Essential to using a GPS is surrendering control. Not long after my first blissful encounter with the GPS, I employed it again, but this time I had trouble giving up control. My teammate and I refused to trust the GPS, and as a result we kept messing things up and losing our way. "Recalculating directions" became a common refrain in the GPS lady's speech.

Losing control can be difficult, yet that is exactly what becoming involves. At the same time, it is not simply about losing our control, but it is about surrendering our control willingly to Jesus. When Jesus called the first disciples, He called them into a relationship that began with a simple invitation to "come." Talk about a lack of instruction! "Come, leave your families and your jobs and everything that is familiar. I'm going to show you a whole new way." Clearly, this relationship required letting go of everything they knew to simply follow Him. I doubt you'll disagree that it still requires this today.

When we let go and begin to follow Jesus, we discover that His way often stands in contrast to our own. Since Jesus is the way, He directs us out of our lostness and sets us rightly on the journey of life in full relationship with Himself. Perhaps you know the feeling of being found when you are lost—there is nothing like it. As a young nineteen-year-old, I knew the emptiness of being lost; I can recall as if it were yesterday that hollow feeling in my gut and that sense of having no purpose or destiny. One night I reached the end of my control over my life, and crying out to God I prayed, If You will forgive me, I will follow You for the rest of my life. My cry for help was a humble one that came as the result of my pride turning into brokenness. It was in my crying out that God heard me and recalculated my direction. A tremendous weight left me that night, as my formerly black-and-white world was illuminated in vivid color. I felt as if I had been dead and had come alive as I experienced His full acceptance and invitation to come follow Him. I had found the Jesus way.

The Becoming Journey

At first, I thought becoming was a destination, but I quickly learned that becoming is really about the journey. God wants to direct our entire path, recalculating our journey when we make a wrong turn or lose our way. God wants to take us to our destiny because He has a plan for our lives. In a recent conversation with my daughter, I was able to tell her, "God has a very special plan for your life, and He doesn't want you to miss it."

This is true for all of us. Unlike the path that many of us plan to take—often the straightest, most direct route—God often chooses the scenic route. It is this path that brings the most value, challenge, beauty, and benefit to our lives, but it is seldom the easiest route. In fact, Jesus described it as the most challenging journey of all: "You can enter God's kingdom only through the narrow gate. The high-way to hell is broad, and its gate is wide for the many who choose that way. But the gateway to life is very narrow and the road is difficult, and only a few ever find it" (Matt. 7:13–14 NLT).

Becoming Is a Relationship

As most relationships develop, we come to know how Jesus lived and loved by watching Him and knowing Him over time, which subsequently sets us up to become like Him. However, for many of us, this relationship can be challenging if we are more familiar with religion than we are with a relationship. Since religion alone is often more about gaining acceptance through what we do, we find ourselves trying to earn the right to relate to God. Like pagans, we constantly try to find ways to appease Him. We think if we can do enough stuff, live up to a certain moral code, discipline ourselves enough, or develop certain spiritual practices, God will be happy with us. The best part about this error in thinking is that we cannot and have not done anything to earn the love of God. He gives it to us because He is good, not because we are good.

Barriers to Becoming

Yet in His goodness, God will not force Himself upon us. We have all erected barriers in our lives that prevent us from becoming like Jesus, and because becoming is about a personal relationship, my barriers are unique to me. At this point in my life, I have found that breaking the discipleship code means losing my religion for religion's sake and following more closely the way of Jesus. The most significant barrier for me has been my tendency to focus more on religion (the things I can do) than on the relationship with Jesus (the things He has done), and my prayer is that He will continue to speak the words "recalculating directions" as I err in my path to live like Him.

I became a follower of Jesus when I was entering my teenage years, and during that time God did much for my family. The transformation was quick and obvious, as God changed our lives as a family and then my life as a person. However, soon afterward I began to experience an inner struggle that was unfamiliar to me. There were temptations in my life that I wasn't accustomed to fighting as someone who had previously lived with no regard for Jesus. I thought something was wrong with me. I remember struggling so hard to live up to what I perceived as God's expectation for me that I grew weary, finally throwing up my hands in defeat. There were times I thought if I couldn't live up to the Christian life, then I wouldn't live it at all. Spiritually, the following five years were the darkest in my life. Mercifully, I later learned how foolish I was as I came to understand God's ways of grace. Precisely as He did not condemn the woman caught in the act of adultery, Jesus did not condemn me—a truth that later came to liberate my life.

The next major barrier to becoming in my life came in my early thirties, as I struggled with the need for approval. I felt I had to meet a certain standard in order to obtain the approval of God and others. When I performed well and experienced success in ministry, everything was good, and I felt I was worthy of love. But when I was struggled with success, as I had defined it according to my own impossibly high standards, I simply wasn't good enough.

As a young pastor, everything I had touched had exceeded my own expectations, as well as those of my leaders. However, later, as I was planting my second church, I found myself constantly dealing with people issues, and the progress was slow. I felt like a failure. Once again, however, it was God's truth that came to liberate me from my own faulty thinking—the truth that I was worthy of the sacrifice of His Son. The truth that He loved me the way I was. The truth that I didn't have to live up to or meet certain expectations to be accepted by Him. This truth set me free.

As is often the case, I was not alone in my experiences. Barriers to becoming are often the results of mind-sets and lifestyle issues that can take a long time to overcome. Often, as relationships with Jesus are begun, that becoming is marked by radical change in which one moment everything seems to be fast and sure, and in the next we've hit a wall. We look down to realize that we are lugging heavy personal baggage into our relationship with Christ, and moving forward has slowed to a crawl. It is not unusual at this point for frustrations to set in, and some even give up.

The good news is that this is part of the process to becoming. If we did not encounter these barriers, we would never be able to overcome them, and our becoming would be severely limited because the journey would lead us to a destiny short of God's plan for our lives. We would be tempted to settle for a religion in which our approval was based on our own accomplishments. Thankfully, that's not the case. Following Jesus is an exciting adventure in becoming that never ends.

The Truth Sets Us Free

Beyond the barriers, we find freedom. In an encounter with Jesus, recorded in the Gospel of John, He clarified this point as the people questioned Him, "'We have never been slaves to anyone. What do you mean, "You will be set free"?' Jesus replied, 'I tell you the truth, everyone who sins is a slave of sin. A slave is not a permanent member of the family, but a son is part of the family forever. So if the Son sets you free, you are truly free'" (John 8:33–36 NLT).

True freedom can come only when we break away from the barriers that so often immobilize us. They take us captive and impede our becoming, but it is in this place that the commitment to truth becomes our liberator. When we study God's Word and allow His Spirit to light up the truth, we find our freedom. If your barrier is legalism, then His truth about grace sets you free; if your barrier is sexual addiction, then His truth about love will ultimately set you free; if your barrier is consumerism, the truth of His sufficiency becomes your sufficiency.

On three different occasions, Jesus was tempted by Satan in the midst of a prolonged fast: first the temptation of hunger, then of glory, and later public power. Each time Satan accosted Him, Jesus lived as the Truth and quoted the words of His Father. Faced with His own limitations as a human, Jesus relied on the truth of the Word of God to sustain Him. It is a commitment to the truth of Jesus that allows us to overcome the barriers we face in becoming (see Matt. 4).

In Real Life

When it comes to shaping and molding us as followers of Jesus, God uses His truth in the context of real life. Although it is rarely (if ever) fun in the moment, God is faithful to turn the outcome into marvelous growth. Consider the following as some of the situations God uses in our lives as He recalculates our direction.

- *God uses pain.* At a certain time in my life, I often found myself in the gym, reminding myself of the old adage "no pain, no gain." No one would argue that God uses the painful parts of life to aid in our becoming like Jesus. For years now I have reflected on James 1:3–4 as a reminder that pain is a sure thing. However, hope is offered as the author goes on to remind us that the benefits that arise out of our pain are often of immeasurable worth: "For you know that when your faith is tested, your endurance has a chance to grow. So let it grow, for when your endurance is fully developed, you will be perfect and complete, needing nothing. If you need wisdom, ask our generous God, and he will give it to you" (NLT).

- *God uses temptation.* The bad news is that temptation is here to stay. We do not arrive at a certain point along the journey of life and find ourselves beyond temptation. It never leaves, and if it abates somewhat, it is only a short time before it arises again. Take comfort, however, in the knowledge that temptation is not sin. We can be tempted, as Jesus was in the desert, and choose not to sin. I love what Rick Warren said in *The Purpose Driven Life:* "Every temptation is an opportunity to do good."³ We can leverage the temptations we face as opportunities to become more like Jesus in the way He lived and loved.

- *God uses my failure.* He really does! Peter is a classic case study, having denied Jesus three times on the night before His crucifixion. He failed—he let down Jesus, his Lord and his very best friend. Many would have succumbed to the belief that all was lost as a result of his failure, but once resurrected, Jesus restored Peter's apostleship, and Peter became the ultimate spokesperson for the early church. Through his failure, he became even stronger and more like Jesus; we are told that the things Jesus did, Peter accomplished even after Jesus's ascension. Even in the midst of his failure, Peter lived like Jesus, loved like Jesus, and ultimately left what Jesus left behind: an entire movement of followers of the Jesus way.

- *God uses time.* I'm still trying to figure things out. I'm still growing, I'm still experiencing, I'm still becoming, and I hope I will continue until my dying day. God has often used the passage of time in my becoming, and I've learned to truly enjoy the journey. Live each day as if it is a new adventure in following Jesus because it is. Growth and becoming like Jesus take time. Know that no matter what comes your way, God uses the gift of time to bring about spiritual maturity and perspective.

Fruit, Not Meat

Jesus tells us in the Gospel of John that becoming like Him is ultimately about bearing fruit: "No branch can bear fruit by itself; it must remain in the vine. Neither can you bear fruit unless you remain in me. I am the vine; you are the branches. If a man remains in me and I in him, he will bear much fruit; apart from me you can do nothing" (John 15:4b–5).

So often we think becoming like Jesus is only about "spiritual meat" or "going deeper." We spend a lot of time in Bible studies characterized by discussions related to our position on the end times and whether Jesus is going to come back before the tribulation, in the middle of the tribulation, or at the end of the tribulation. I'm not saying these discussions don't have their place, but when conversations like that dominate our time and our consciousness, we fail to leave room for cultivating the fruit of our faith. We forget to live and love like Jesus.

But fruit is not the object of our faith; fruit is the result of becoming, and it is the natural consequence of our connection to the Vine. The spiritual fruit we bear reflects the work of the Spirit in us; thus, it's called the fruit of the Spirit: "love, joy, peace, patience, kindness, goodness, faithfulness, gentleness and self-control" (Gal. 5:22b–23a). The appearance of fruit in our lives is what becoming is all about. When the Holy Spirit works in us to cultivate this result, we will find we are living the life of a missional follower of Jesus.

A Chair and a Cup of Coffee

Jesus said that I cannot bear fruit unless I remain in Him (John 15:4). For me, becoming is really about learning to live in His presence, hearing Him, following Him, obeying Him. The challenge with this simple task, however, is that I often run in my own direction and lose my way. It seems so much easier to do it my way, but when I attempt to live this way, I fail to see His kingdom because I am so full of my own kingdom.

That's why recalculating direction begins, for me, with my chair and a cup of coffee. My mind and my life run at about one hundred miles an hour, and I need a place where I can slow down . . . settle down . . . get down . . . to hear and see God. Therefore, my chair is my place to meet God regularly and to see His perspective in my life. Over time I have learned to live in His presence constantly, allowing this presence to invade my life throughout the day. But even still, my time in the morning in my chair with my coffee sets the tone for each day.

Because I believe that following Jesus is about a relationship, I begin my day with Jesus by doing what I often do with good friends: have a cup of coffee and enjoy His company. I once preached a message and brought my chair onto the stage to demonstrate this daily ritual. One individual became very angry with me for modeling an approach to God so casual and relational, but more often than not, I think people have enough religious ritual in their lives and can benefit from a little more simplicity.

My time with Jesus also requires a few other things.

My Bible

In addition to my coffee, when I sit in my chair I also have my Bible. I love my Bible. I don't understand everything in it, and I am finally OK with that. There are some things I am going to have to ask God about when I get to heaven. But I do trust my Bible and believe that it is one of the primary ways God speaks to me. As a matter of fact, I believe that anything I think I hear God saying to me should be run through the filter of the Bible. I have heard followers of Jesus suggest some of the strangest things in an effort to justify their actions. We need the Bible to guide us through life. Where else can we discover the Jesus way?

When I am occupying my chair in the mornings, I use my Bible in several different ways. Sometimes I read and meditate on one certain part of it. I especially like to read the Sermon on the Mount and others of Jesus's public teachings because they are a great example to me as I follow Jesus. When I read other parts of the Scriptures, aside from the Gospels, I always filter what I read through the words of Jesus.

Another way I read the Bible—or maybe a better way of putting it is the way the Bible reads me—is through what I call life verses. Through the years I have found that specific passages in the Bible always go straight to my heart. I can't read these verses without being significantly impacted, and I enjoy spending time with a singular focus on these passages. These Scriptures never get old to me, and I never tire of reading them. They have become part of me.

I have had the good fortune to have been a follower of Jesus for a number of years, and through the years I have become familiar with the Bible as one becomes familiar with one's house. Although I don't visit every part of my house every day, I know it inside and out. When I'm looking for something specific, I might not remember which box I put it in, but I do know that it is in one of the four boxes in the closet under the steps.

Similarly, I have discovered there are certain passages of Scripture I use more regularly that are always at the forefront of my mind, exactly as I keep certain things displayed in my house in more prominent locations. One of those Scriptures is the passage on the fruit of the Spirit I mentioned earlier. This Scripture passage has grabbed hold of me and will not let go, and I love to concentrate on it as I am sitting in my chair. I think this is part of the journey. God plants His Word in our hearts, and over time He grows a garden of soul food.

My Journal

In addition to my Bible, I have a Moleskine journal that I keep with me. There are a lot of things I love about my journal—I like the way it bends in the middle so I can write on both sides of the page with equal ease. I also like that the pages inside are laid out with a grid; I hate staying between the lines, so the grids allow me to start my thoughts anywhere I want on the paper, and they also allow me to draw pictures to express my thoughts. Since much of my time with God is spent trying to see what God is doing around and in me, I spend a fair part of my time drawing diagrams of what I see. Most mornings when I open my journal, I write out my prayers, a few thoughts that seem most urgent, and the theme of my conversation with God that day.

Another thing my journal has become over time is a place where I integrate much of my life. Early in my journal keeping, I considered it a holy place that needed to be kept in precise order. I would write my prayers almost to completion, and I would write a few key Scriptures and a goal or two. Today, my journal is more a reflection of my life—I don't have my grocery list in it but nearly everything else. If I have an important thought, I write it down. If I say or do something related to those thoughts, I write that down as well. If I have a writing idea, I write it down. If I think of something that will impact our church or ministry, I write it down. There are times when I plan in my journal, write sermons, or outline my next resource for church planters. On special occasions I write notes to my children in my journal and later convey that note verbally. I write nearly anything and everything in my journal, and it is a reflection of my life: messy and all over the place. I love it.

A Good Book

I love to read books written by people who are also on a journey to becoming. When I read their stories, God really speaks to me from their experiences. This doesn't happen every time I pick up a book, but often, in addition to reading my Bible, I take out one of these books and meditate on the truth that comes from it.

These are some of the practices I employ to center my life on becoming; what you do to connect with God may look completely different. Understand I have found these ways to help me become more like Christ, and it looks different from time to time. Set out to determine your own methods and practices over time. What speaks to you? What really works for you? The important thing is that we center our lives on Jesus daily.

A Road Map

The beauty of our GPS friend in Chicago was that it was a road map complete with intuition. The specific path you take in your route to becoming will look different from everyone else's, but you can ask yourself questions to evaluate your progress. Let me suggest five that may be helpful.

1. *Am I growing in my personal relationship with Jesus?* It is the responsibility of every follower of Jesus to grow spiritually. Am I taking the personal responsibility to grow in my relationship with Jesus? If I am, it will be characterized by time with Him and the fruit of the Spirit. A serious misunderstanding people have is that it is the responsibility of a paid preacher or teacher to bring about this kind of spiritual growth. However, we know from life that every growing child becomes more autonomous every day. The same is true for our spiritual lives. If we are sitting back in our pews saying, "Feed me, feed me," this is an indication something is wrong. Going back to my earlier definition of what a

follower of Jesus is, am I living, loving, and leaving what Jesus left behind? To grow spiritually is to become like Him.

2. *Am I serving others as Jesus served?* When I speak of using my gifts, I am not necessarily referring to the endless number of spiritual gift inventories that exist to tell me what my gift mix is, but I am referring to the specific, singular gift that Jesus modeled in His last supper with the disciples: "Jesus knew that the Father had put all things under his power, and that he had come from God and was returning to God; so he got up from the meal, took off his outer clothing, and wrapped a towel around his waist. After that, he poured water into a basin and began to wash his disciples' feet, drying them with the towel that was wrapped around him" (John 13:3–5).

Using our gifts begins with the heart and learning to serve others. I believe that one of the marks of growth as a follower of Jesus is that we grow in our service and discover new gifts and new ways of using those gifts. In what ways are you intentionally humbling yourself in service to other people?

3. *Am I experiencing community at the level of belonging?* Jesus clearly demonstrated the necessity of community in how He lived and loved, as He explained the Great Commandment to love God and love people. I will say this over and over again: Jesus came into this world to call us into healthy relationships with God and others. We were designed to be part of one another. If we are to truly become like Jesus, we must engage not only in a community of believers but in community with those outside the church. Read the Gospels and see that much of Jesus's time was spent in meaningful community, whether with His followers or with those who knew very little about Him.

4. *Am I becoming more about His kingdom in the way I view and use my resources?* Is Jesus getting more of me today than He did yesterday? Becoming is reflected in the way we view our possessions and our motivations for putting them to use in His kingdom. When I give of myself with a vision for impacting His kingdom, I am on the right track to becoming. On the other hand, when I find myself holding on to everything for myself, I realize that life has become all about me and I have forgotten my place as a steward of God's resources.

5. *Am I seeing my influence and impact in the kingdom grow?* Jesus was serious about having increased impact. He was the friend of sinners who had come to seek and save the lost. He came to die that we might be influenced and changed. His last instructions in the Great Commission were to go into the world to impact it with His message (Matt. 28:19–20). Everything we do in our local churches should be leveraged to have greater impact in the world. It's the natural overflow of being a follower of Jesus.

Whose Voice Is That?

Learning to listen is essential in navigating the Jesus way. As we have to listen to our GPS in order to arrive at our destination, we must learn to listen to Jesus if we are going to follow His way. The amazing thing is He is always with us. He promised us His Spirit and His presence through His Spirit to the very end of the age: "The watchman opens the gate for him, and the sheep listen to his voice. He calls his own sheep by name and leads them out. When he has brought out all his own, he goes on ahead of them, and his sheep follow him because they know his voice. But they will never follow a stranger; in fact, they will run away from him because they do not recognize a stranger's voice" (John 10:3–5).

Becoming a follower of Jesus is about hearing His voice and following Him. Jesus is with us always. Becoming is about decreasing ourselves so He might increase in our lives. That's right—more of Jesus and less of us.

Feeding Ourselves

Recently, leaders of Willowcreek Community Church, one of the most influential churches, went on record saying they had made a mistake assuming activity would produce spiritual growth. It just didn't happen. Bill Hybels, the lead pastor, confessed, "We made a mistake. What we should have done when people crossed the line of faith and became Christians, we should have started telling people and teaching people that they have to take responsibility to become 'self-feeders.'"[4]

Let's face it. We have all made mistakes when it comes to becoming. Often we have supplemented our becoming with activities. We, too, could benefit from confession and allowing God to recalculate our directions. Perhaps the centerpiece of our journey should be less about an activity and more about our time with Jesus, getting to know him and his ways. Go ahead, grab a cup of coffee and settle in your chair. Listen closely to what God is saying to you through His Word.

Something to Think About

1. When it comes to becoming, what barriers in your life are holding you back?
2. How can truth help you overcome these barriers?
3. Describe your plan for allowing God to recalculate directions in your life on a daily basis.
4. Conduct an evaluation of your life, using the five questions under the section titled "A Road Map." What are your next steps in becoming?

While Jesus was having dinner at Levi's house, many tax
collectors and "sinners" were eating with him and his disciples, . . .
When the teachers of the law who were Pharisees saw him . . . , they
asked his disciples: "Why does he eat with tax collectors and 'sinners'?"
On hearing this, Jesus said to them, "It is not the healthy who need a
doctor, but the sick. I have not come to call the righteous, but sinners."

—MARK 2:15–17

CHAPTER 8

Going: Becoming a Friend of Sinners

When I was nineteen, I had seriously lost my way and needed help in finding it. That's when I met A. C. Running out of options and really being desperate, I stumbled back to my roots and landed in church. In hindsight I thank God that I grew up familiar with the church so that I would turn there during my later teen years. I attended most Sunday morning services, but I often sat there daydreaming about my weekend. I'm not sure why I went, but being there made me feel better because it gave me a kind of hope.

But with a single connection inside that community of believers, things began to change for me. A. C. was an older guy in the church who took time to seek me out. He came up to me and said, "David, God has laid you on my heart. We have a group of younger boys from the neighborhood who could probably relate to you. They come to the church on Monday nights, and I would like you to consider coming and helping out with them. We just hang out and play ball and stuff like that." This blew my mind.

For a young man trying to find his way back to God, this was good news. I really thought I had crossed an invisible line in my life where there was no chance of getting back to God; I thought my story was finished. But I remember thinking that if A. C. was right and God had put me on his heart, maybe it wasn't too late. I started showing up at the church campus on Monday nights and saw that it had become a gathering spot for boys of all ages from our community. Through my volunteering with these rowdy boys, I began to find my way back to Jesus, and after weeks and months I began to reconnect with Him. It wasn't much longer until I invited Jesus into my journey and I hit a new gear in my growth. If it hadn't been for A. C. and his unorthodox way of serving, I think I might still be searching.

That was only the beginning. A little later, I ran into Barry, an old friend of mine. He had lost his way, too, but his errors had landed him in jail. In our younger days, Barry and I had gotten in a lot of trouble together. As I pulled into the gas station one afternoon, there he was. We quickly reconnected, and the first thing out of his mouth was, "What have you been up to?" Before I could stop myself, I began explaining to him, "Barry, to be completely honest with you, I've been up to a lot. I've found God." With a surprised look, Barry responded, "You did what?" As I went on to explain, I braced for Barry's incredulous response, but he completely threw me off guard by saying instead, "That's what I want! I want to find God! Can you help me?"

So I did the only thing I knew to do. I told him about the boys I volunteered with on Monday nights and how I had been hanging out with them and in the process had found God. I told him I thought he should do the same thing, and sure enough, Barry started helping out with those rowdy boys on Monday nights, and it wasn't long before he found God too. I still recall with amazing clarity the night he prayed for Jesus to forgive him and to help him find his way. It was so sweet and so humbling to see Barry finding his way again.

I tell this story because I don't know where I would be if A. C. had not met me in my search and invited me into his acceptance.

I needed help and A. C. became my unofficial guide. Later, not even knowing it, I became Barry's unofficial guide, and in time Barry went on to guide others. In a matter of months we saw many of our friends find the way to Jesus. It was an awesome time in all of our lives. The amazing thing is that we weren't familiar with the Great Commission, and we certainly weren't trained in any methods of personal evangelism. However, as we went through life, we left a wake of changed lives as we lived our stories with gratitude and excitement.

Friend of Sinners

This reminds me of one of my favorite stories in the Bible, the story of Matthew. Matthew was a tax collector, which, in biblical times, meant he was about as low down as you could be. Not only did he accept taxes on behalf of Caesar, which was considered treason, he also took a little extra for himself. He was a well-dressed, well-paid thief who took people's money and suffered no consequences. He was hated above all other officials, yet Jesus risked His own reputation to spend time with Matthew, eat with him, and even invite him to be one of His disciples. Matthew explains: "When the Pharisees saw this, they asked his disciples, 'Why does your teacher eat with tax collectors and "sinners"?' On hearing this, Jesus said, 'It is not the healthy who need a doctor, but the sick. . . . For I have not come to call the righteous, but sinners'" (9:11–13).

Jesus was a friend to sinners, and this is the key to His Great Commission. Jesus genuinely loved people and not only people who were like Him or people who agreed with Him. He loved the tax collectors, the prostitutes, the thieves, the poor, the sick—everyone. It was this love that moved Him to become a friend of sinners.

Agnes Liu discovered what it meant to become a friend of sinners when she became concerned for the factory workers in Hong Kong. Understanding that Christianity in Hong Kong was primarily a middle-class movement, she left her job as a seminary professor and went to work as a seamstress in a factory. As a coworker and friend, she became familiar with them in every way. In essence, she became one of them, and as she befriended her coworkers over time, many of them became Christians. Here is what she discovered about their journey: Before becoming Christ followers, they typically viewed the church as boring and did not like most Christians. Once they met and became friends with a Christian, they were open to attending church; and once they did, they found it to be OK. From there, increasingly they began to live like Jesus, and over time became followers of Jesus.[5]

Our Christian Subculture

On the other hand, some barriers keep us from becoming friends of sinners and ultimately fulfilling the Great Commission. One is our Christian subculture. Whether or not we believe it, we often act as if we should keep our lives separated from those who are not followers of Jesus, and if we play it safe enough and stay separated enough, we will never have to worry about anyone accusing us of hanging out with sinners. My wife was recently invited to join a social networking Web site devoted solely to Christians. I couldn't believe it—a place where we Christians can go and not be tarnished by the world. No wonder there is an image barrier when it comes to how disconnected people perceive us. It reminds me of the story in the Bible in which Jesus took John, Peter, and James up a mountain and was transfigured before them as He spoke with Moses and Elijah. What did they want to do? They wanted to build a holy space there and never leave the mountain again. I love Jesus's response: "Get up" (Matt. 17:7b).

What are we thinking? Jesus was clear when He said, "Get up." We Christians have got to wake up and realize that life is not all about us. It should not be our goal to open our eyes every day thinking about how we can gather more Christians into a space and protect ourselves from the outside world.

I later had a conversation with the creator of that particular Web site in which he explained that he created it to provide an alternative to similar sites on the Internet that are filled with dangerous images and content. To be fair, his is a valid point, but I think even something as mundane as a Web presence can become a ministry for being a friend to sinners.

Admittedly, I understand this struggle. Somewhere down the line I, too, was under the impression that good Christians didn't hang out with sinners. I don't know where that reasoning came from; it certainly was not the Bible. While I was in seminary, the company my wife worked for at the time held a blowout Christmas party. It was an incredible evening, complete with an endless buffet of food and drink. From my experience at the time, there was nothing wrong with gorging oneself on the food, but a good Christian did not even go into the same room with alcohol. But, to my amazement, while I was there something began to happen: I discovered that it wasn't as bad as I thought it would be. I began to meet people and engage in meaningful conversations with many of them, and by mealtime the party was in full swing.

That's when the president of the company caught me off guard by introducing me to the entire company as Tami's husband and a pastor. I hate it when that happens because it causes instant barriers to rise. He went on to ask me to pray for the meal, so I prayed a very quick, sincere prayer with no fancy words or religious phrasing. I prayed for a good evening and safe return home, and I thanked God for Jesus. But I can't really explain what happened next—it was one of those unexplainable God moments. When I said, "Amen," everyone in the room broke out in applause. I had become their friend, and they were celebrating with me the hope of Jesus. Later I would go on to lead a Bible study in that company because some of the executive leadership wanted to learn more about the Bible. The barriers were broken down when I got over my own religious barriers and began taking seriously Jesus's attitude toward sinners.

Let me add that I believe this truth alone could revolutionize our impact with people who are disconnected from Jesus and the church. One of our most common problems is that because of our Christian subculture, we really don't know anyone who isn't already a Christian. If we do, we probably stay away from him or her. Imagine what would happen if we all became friends of sinners. Something tells me this is all it would take to make a huge impact in the world.

Barrier of Church Structure

I also believe that our busyness has become a barrier to those outside the church. We are so busy creating this protective Christian social club that if by some chance we felt compelled to become a friend to sinners, we simply would not have the time or energy to do so.

My first experiences with church kept me so busy that I didn't have time to invest in any relationship, much less friendships outside the church. I now wonder if this was not by design. Oh sure, we had lots of ministries to the community, which was a good thing; but by the time I attended church on Sunday morning and evening, attended a midweek prayer service, and showed up for a formal visitation program, I had no time for my own family much less to become a friend to sinners. I wonder what would have happened if I had spent less time doing outreach projects and more time hanging out with sinners. Today, things are largely still the same. Although our structures may have become simplified, our lifestyles have become busier and more complicated.

Today, I am a pastor in a church that has taken seriously our programming structure as a barrier. We do only two things a week that require attendance: weekend worship and weekday small groups. Our worship services happen on our campus, while all of our groups take place in homes throughout the community. At the same time, even with such simple programming, it is amazing how quickly our schedules can fill up with church stuff. Before we know it, we simply don't have the time or energy to connect with people outside our churches.

Going and Coming

I love the story known as the woman at the well (John 4:1–42). Jesus went to her and began a conversation that resulted in her going back to her village and bringing many people out to meet Him. For Jesus, it was a matter of "going and telling," while for the woman it was a matter of "coming and seeing." It is an amazing story when you look at it. Here was someone who had no prior knowledge of or relationship with Jesus. Yet, she encountered Him and became the key influence in bringing an entire village to Him.

I see this happening all the time in our church. Every week new people come, and they come because someone has invited them. Regular attenders (and often first-time attenders) are going and telling, sometimes without even knowing they are going. They have witnessed for themselves the healing, fulfilling work of Jesus; and out of the overflow of their relationship, they go and tell others about their experience. Others go and tell even though they are not sure if what they have found is the truth. They think they may be on to something, and they experience a sense of hope, so they tell others. Many times they bring their friends and families back, and they continue the search together. It is not unusual to see entire households and entire networks of relationships find Jesus all at once.

When we go and tell, a natural effect is that we invite people to come and see. The question, however, is that when we invite them to come and see, where do we invite them to? I know our motive for inviting them is to put them in a position to see Jesus, but where do we find Jesus? For many of us this means inviting them into our lives. We become a friend of sinners. We live and we love people as Jesus lived and loved people. However, at the same time, it's not enough merely to invite them into our lives; it is an incomplete picture of Jesus.

Where do we invite them? We invite them into the family, for we are a family. We invite them into the body because we are the body and we are incomplete on our own. We invite them to the wedding, for we are the bride and Jesus is the bridegroom. One is not complete without the other, and the marriage is beautiful.

While the church takes on many forms in today's world, we are still one church. We are the family, the body, that radiant bride, and as that beautiful expression of Christ, what better place to come and see? For too long our churches have been for members only, but I believe that, today, that is changing in many ways. It is challenging to all of us; but it is an important transition because as God has called us to go and tell, He also has called us to invite others to come and see.

This is why it is crucial that we as churches go missional every time we meet by providing safe, inviting places for people to come and see. Rampant among church leaders is a debate whether we are to be missional, as when we are going and telling others about Jesus, or attractional, as when we are inviting others to come and see. This is a destructive argument because the reality is that it takes both. The healthiest churches have a working strategy for reaching out into their surrounding regions as well as a commitment to maintaining a welcoming environment in the setting of the church community itself. Both are essential, and when the two methods come together, there is a tremendous synergy that results in life change for all involved.

Live Your Story

A very short time ago, a good friend of my daughter's passed away; in fact, they had dated for the previous year, attended the same college, and were truly best friends. Sam, only twenty years old, was a cancer survivor. The summer before his death, Sam had a ribbon tattooed on the back of his shoulder that read, "Fightin' until the last breath," and Sam fought and lived, indeed, until his very last breath. The day before he was scheduled for surgery, he went to a baseball game with some of his friends, where they took lots of great photos of silly stuff. They arrived home late but were having too much fun to sleep, so they stayed up talking, laughing, and playing the PlayStation until 1:30 a.m. The next morning Sam and his family went to the hospital for his surgery, where the last thing Sam said to his mom was, "Don't stand there looking so sad. I will be back in a little bit. Go make a new friend." That after-noon Sam died on the operating table during a surgery designed to remove a mass in his chest.

Since battling cancer for the first time at the age of fifteen, Sam fought a good fight, often giving his time to serving and loving others fighting the same disease. It was not unusual for me to ask my daughter, "Where's Sam?" to which she would respond, "He's at the hospital visiting the kids." The week after his death, he was scheduled to serve as a counselor at a camp for children with cancer. I listened to his parents as they talked about how Sam had picked up a young girl with a brain tumor, wheelchair and all, and danced with her. Sam was a big, athletic kid. I can see him dancing now.

I want to be like Sam. I believe he was more like Jesus when he picked up that young girl than most of us ever get the chance to be. Sam had a story, and he lived it. We all have a story, and although our stories may all be different, we can all go and tell the story of how Jesus came into our lives and brought new meaning and purpose out of our pain, suffering, and sin. Let this be the starting block for your mission of going and telling. It does not have to be complicated. My story is of a kid growing up with little or no hope in the home of an alcoholic dad whose entire family eventually came to Jesus. My wife's story centers on being hit by a van and recovering, not only in a physical sense but recovering with a new meaning and purpose. My daughter's story will now be filled with a chapter from Sam's life that will greatly shape her heart for a missional life of going and telling.

I love the ancient story of Joseph told in Genesis. When he had suffered for many years because of his brothers and finally had the opportunity to repay them, his story took an odd shift when he said, "Don't be afraid. Am I in the place of God? You intended to harm me, but God intended it for good to accomplish what is now being done, the saving of many lives" (Gen. 50:19–20). Wherever we find ourselves and in whatever circumstances, when we allow Jesus to saturate our stories, they become stories worth telling.

The Things Jesus Began

The account of the church, told in the book of Acts, begins with these words: "In my former book, Theophilus, I wrote about all that Jesus began to do and to teach" (Acts 1:1). In other words, the Gospels tell the stories of Jesus's work on earth, and as recounted in the book of Acts, the first church continued those things Jesus began to do and teach. Jesus continued His work through His disciples, but even now He continues through us. Once you've witnessed the work of Jesus in and around your life and your story, you can hardly keep yourself from continuing to go and tell that story.

I once got a phone call from a large national organization that wanted to know what kind of program we used, as a church, to get people to go into their communities and further the mission of Jesus. He was surprised when I told him we didn't have one. I went on to describe how we sought to make the church the missionary in our community, and still he seemed to struggle with what I was telling him. He suggested that perhaps we were reaching only people who were already believers, but I assured him it was really quite the opposite. All I know is that when you are committed to becoming a missional follower of Jesus by living like Him and loving like Him, you are going to naturally leave what He left behind, which is more people who live and love like Jesus.

This is the story of the church.

Don't merely have church; be the church. It will make all the difference.

Something to Think About

1. Are you afraid of associating with persons disconnected from Jesus and the church? Describe how this affects your journey.

2. Make a list of those disconnected from Jesus and the church in whom you are investing relationally.

3. What does partnering with your local church in being a friend of sinners look like?

4. What is your story? How does that story connect with your call to go?

Book 3

What Does a Missional Follower of Jesus Look Like?

What does it mean to have integrity as a missional follower of Jesus? If you look at the etymology of *integrity,* it comes from the word *integer,* a whole number or a complete unit. The idea that best represents integrity as it relates to being a follower of Jesus is "the quality or condition of being whole or undivided; completeness."[6] It is when that which is on the inside and the outside are the same. They are fully integrated. What you see is what you get. So when it is said that one has integrity, it is to say that there is a kind of wholeness and completeness about that person's life; he or she moves through life with ease and grace.

One reason I wrote this part of the book is that I rarely see this kind of ease and grace when it comes to following Jesus. What I do see is a one-dimensional approach to following Jesus that often does more harm than good. We know how to live and love at church or in our own religious subcultures, at least most of the time, but when it comes to being a missional follower of Jesus in a way that takes us outside the church, we often lack the wherewithal to develop meaningful relationships and interaction. We are clumsy and awkward. Therefore, instead of meaningful engagement, we choose to sit on the sidelines or within the safety net of our religious subcultures. At the same time, we are called to live in this world as missional followers of Jesus. It is my prayer that the discussions arising from this book will begin the journey to wholeness for those who read it.

Any discussion of the ways in which we are called to engage the world can only scratch the surface of the complexity we live in. The thoughts that follow are bred from my experiences, but there are countless other scenarios I would have loved to address. While I've tried to be reasonably comprehensive, I may not have touched on the scenario that best describes your life. The truth is, we all are writing a book with our lives, and it is the story of God's work. Move forward in your story of wholeness by examining your own situation in light of the gospel. Consider not necessarily what Jesus would have done but what He did. Maybe He wasn't in a position on a church board and didn't work as an accountant or raise children, but He lived and loved in a way that is transferable to any situation. Such love compels us to emulate Him in every circumstance of our lives.

"For where your treasure is, there your heart will be also."
—MATTHEW 6:21

What Does a Missional Follower Look Like in Our Churches?

Looking back, I probably should have seen it coming, but that day seemed like a great day to shop for a car. My consumer instincts were flying high. My ten-year-old Jeep was approaching 150,000 miles and making large deposits of oil on my concrete driveway every time I parked it. I knew it was on its last leg. I had waited as long as I could, but it was time for a replacement. I had been tracking auto prices in the newspaper for several weeks, and that morning I found an advertisement for a nearby dealership that seemed to be too good to be true (again, I should have seen it coming). I asked my teenage daughter if she wanted to join me, knowing, but not revealing that I was aware, of her vested interest in the potential new car and the chance that I would ultimately pass it down to her.

As we drove around that afternoon, I reinforced to her (and myself) that I was only planning to look—not purchase—and I really meant it. As we entered the dealership and were introduced to a salesman, I clearly stated my objective. I explained to the eager salesman that I would probably buy a new vehicle in the next month but only after I had done a fair amount of research. I also explained that I never bought a car on sight. He seemed to understand my terms, and he listened to my predetermined criteria for a new car before driving us around the sprawling dealership in a golf cart. When we found a vehicle I liked and felt would meet my needs, the salesman told me he would get a price for me. I gently reminded him that I was only looking and that under no circumstances was I prepared to purchase a vehicle that day. We seemed to have a good understanding, so he returned to his office to find the price. In a few minutes he came back with a number written on a piece of paper and said, "Mr. Putman, I can't believe it. We have never offered a deal like this before." Showing me the price, he went on to say, "Mr. Putman, with a deal like this, what is it going to take to finalize this right now?"

You might imagine my surprise at his lack of understanding of our previous conversation. I thought I had been clear. I kindly explained that the information he provided gave me everything I needed to make a decision, and I told him that I would give the matter some consideration and return in a few days. He quickly responded, "I understand, but wait right here for just a moment." He returned with another gentleman who was also under the impression that I could be made to purchase a car that day. To my astonishment, this second salesman said, "Mr. Putman, I understand you want to buy a vehicle. What do we need to do to put you in that vehicle today?" Being as nice as I could be, I reiterated my earlier conversation with his colleague and told him that I would not be buying a vehicle that day. I'm not sure what it was about our conversation he didn't understand. He continued to press, and I continued to grow more frustrated. Once more I informed them that I had no plans to purchase a car from them that day, and my daughter and I walked out.

This whole experience really bugged me. I was bugged that he didn't get it. I was bugged that this whole experience had brought out the worst in me. As I thought about the exchange in the following days, it occurred to me that the salespeople were so deafened by their desire to sell that they hadn't heard a word I had said. Even though I would be purchasing the vehicle for my use, the transaction had become all about them.

It is like God to use an exchange like this to teach me something. As I reflect on this experience, I realize that when it comes to following Him, it often becomes about me. The truth is, it's not only me this happens to. When it comes to the church and our mission, it is so easy to think it is all about us. We are often deafened and blinded to the needs of those around us. We see them without seeing them; we hear them without hearing them. We choose our churches using our own preferences—what is closest to our house, how well we relate to the teaching style, and how much we enjoy the worship. And once we find a church for us, we forget about them— those who aren't already connected to Jesus and the church. And I'm as guilty as anyone; I often think this life is about me—what I want, what I need, my preferences, and my desires.

Jesus confronted these same issues with the Pharisees of His day. In many ways they most resemble us as consumerist Americans in that they were consumers of religious goods and services. They held high positions in the church and the community, they were religiously in touch, they had influence and power, they were concerned about protecting their community, they were rich with their traditions, and they seemed to be satisfied with the way things were. They had created the perfect utopia for themselves and those close to them.

Within this context Jesus displayed one of the most seemingly incongruous moments of His ministry when He approached the temple during the Passover, a time of spiritual celebration. We are told in Mark 11 of this exchange: "Jesus entered the temple area and began driving out those who were buying and selling there. He overturned the tables of the money changers and the benches of those selling doves, and would not allow anyone to carry merchandise through the temple courts. And as He taught them, He said, 'Is it not written: "My house will be called a house of prayer for all nations"? But you have made it a den of robbers'" (vv. 15–17).

This is an interesting passage of Scripture. We often settle for discussions related to Jesus's anger and miss the point. In actuality, the changing of money and the selling of doves were common and acceptable practices in Jerusalem. These sales enabled people coming from miles and miles away to participate in worship by purchasing their sacrificial animals in Jerusalem rather than bringing them along on an arduous journey to the temple. It was actually a good thing to offer these animals for sale to pilgrims. The problem Jesus addressed was where these transactions were taking place: What was normally reserved for outside the temple had made its way into the outer court of the temple. The outer court was a place where no one was excluded from God. It was a place where there were no barriers, where those who had the greatest need could come and meet God, and it was the only place where non-Jews could worship. So why did Jesus get so angry? As if things were not convenient enough, the market had been moved into the outermost court of the temple. Thus, Jesus said, "Is it not written: 'My house will be called a house of prayer for all nations'? But you have made it a den of robbers." The problem wasn't the resource table; it was where the Jewish officials had set it up. Their carelessness in making it convenient for them had become a barrier to a specific group of people; they had made worship an experience all about them rather than those coming to worship who truly feared God.

The temples and synagogues of Jesus's day, and later the early church, were incredible tools for leveraging the gospel in Jesus's world. The church provided one of the means in which rapid multiplication of Christ followers was possible. We need the church in North America and all over the world, along with all of the followers of Jesus who live and serve in them, to rise and join together in living like Jesus and loving like Jesus. If the church is to be the church as Jesus intended it, we must remember that the church is not all about me and it's not all about you—Jesus never intended for it to become a religious country club. The church exists for others.

The primary danger in believing that the church exists for me is the threat of becoming a consumer of church. As consumers, we spend our resources on ourselves—our interests, our needs, our wants, and our pleasures. And not only do we spend our resources on our needs and wants; we even spend the resources we "give away" on ourselves: Often the resources we give to our local churches are spent mainly on providing religious services for ourselves. Face it: we are consumers by nature, having been born into the lap of constant consumption as Americans. Not only do we consume the majority of our world's natural, technological, and entertainment resources, we spend the majority of the world's religious resources on ourselves as well. We have built larger and more expensive buildings, even though church attendance is down.[7] We have spent more money on educating our preachers and teachers, even though we complain that they are boring and irrelevant. We build and maintain the best Christian schools and colleges, even though our kids are leaving the faith. We build the most elaborate denominational systems and buildings, even though our denominations are shrinking.

At the same time, there is an epidemic of AIDS in Third-World countries around the globe. Our urban centers are overrun with illiteracy problems, teenage pregnancies, fatherless homes, abused welfare systems, gangs, violence, poverty, and crime. Natural disasters have destroyed our land, and our neighbors are struggling to find even the dimmest glimmer of hope.

All about Me?

Could it be that the god that most competes with us as followers of Jesus is the god of consumerism? Have we become consumers of religious goods and our churches vendors of religious services? Alan Hirsch certainly thinks so. In his book *The Forgotten Ways* he wrote, "Ninety percent or more of the people who attend our services are passive. In other words, they are consumptive. They are the passive recipients of the religious goods and services being delivered largely by professionals in a slick presentation and service. Just about everything we do in these somewhat standardized services and 'box churches,' we do in order to attract participants, and to do this we need to make the experience of church more convenient and comfortable. It is the ultimate religious version of one-stop-hassle-free shopping."[8]

Ouch! Have we displaced Jesus from our churches, replacing Him with our need to consume religious products and services? Could He really be outside the church knocking, seeking entry? I must confess that this hits a little too close to home for my liking. In many ways I think Hirsch is right—we pour in on the weekend and participate in a worship service that is easy to consume. However, before we dismiss all of our churches that haven't transitioned to coffee tables and houses, we need to look deeper. Any structure or form can become about my need to worship a god of consumption. I'm convinced that any church, no matter when we meet or what we look like, can make a difference when Jesus is on the inside.

When He is inside, something wonderful happens to all of our activities. Our worship becomes true worship. Our giving becomes true sacrifice. Our going becomes infused with power. Our sense of community takes on a deep sense of belonging. Our serving takes on a selfless act of gratitude. Our love becomes self-sacrificing. Our giving becomes a reflection of His heart.

Our churches become the body of Christ.

What If . . . ?

What if we began to reconsider our religious consumption? What if we thought about it in ways similar to our consumption of our natural resources? What if we saw our tendency to consume as one of the major ways we, as the church, have lost our way and really began to rethink our way of living? What if we confessed that we have made our churches and the whole idea of following Jesus cater to our own desires? I believe this could lead to a whole new way of living.

I met a guy at a party one night who really got me thinking. During our conversation he made a statement I imagine he has long since forgotten. It was one of those statements that grabbed hold of me and has not let go. Here is what he said: "I'm doing well and my business is good, but I've chosen to live below my means." For some reason it never occurred to me until that minute that I could live below my means. What if we, as followers of Jesus, made this kind of commitment? What if we made a decision like this with respect to the houses we live in, the meals we eat, the vacations we take, the clothes we buy, and the education we achieve? What if we decided to make decisions about consumption based on a set of kingdom values that fly in the face of cultural norms? But, what if we didn't stop there? What if we always gave back more then we consumed? What if we adopted a minimalist mentality about all of life? God has given us so much. What if we spent most of our lives trying to give back?

Consumption?

Our temptation is to avoid this discussion altogether. We want to ask the question, What does consumption have to do with it? If we are serious about living like Jesus and loving like Jesus, the answer is everything. Jesus put it this way: "No one can serve two masters. Either he will hate the one and love the other, or he will be devoted to the one and despise the other. You cannot serve both God and Money" (Matt. 6:24).

At another time, a young rich man came to Jesus asking Him what he must do to really experience life on earth and the life after.

The young man was a very religious man who had kept all the commandments, yet Jesus went a step further when He told him, "If you want to be perfect, go, sell your possessions and give to the poor, and you will have treasure in heaven. Then come follow me" (Matt. 19:21). The story concludes with the rich young man going away sorrowful because he wasn't willing to give up his riches.

Jesus is clear that if we want to live and love like Him, we have to be willing to give up everything to follow Him. He goes to great lengths to demonstrate and communicate that my life is not about me, but it is about Him and others. "Sell your possessions and give to the poor." What a radical teaching. Practically speaking, consider the following ways to reduce your spiritual consumption or to dethrone your god of consumption.

- *Get involved with a church that has a vision for the world.*

I believe in the church. Jesus died for the church, and He has chosen to work through the church as His body in this world. I have given my whole life to the church, and I'm glad I have. However, it is easy for the church as a whole, as it is for individuals, to get caught up in our own agendas, determined to fulfill our own desires. I was visiting a church on Easter a number of years ago and realized that the name of Jesus wasn't mentioned one time in the service. I was struck with the image that John described in the third chapter of Revelation, when Jesus said, "Here I am! I stand at the door and knock. If anyone hears my voice and opens the door, I will go in and eat with him, and he with me" (v. 20). It is easy for me to point my finger at my experience that Sunday; however, I, too, am guilty of leaving Jesus outside the church. Perhaps one of the greatest challenges for the church today is to rediscover the centrality of Jesus—opening the door and letting Him back in.

At the same time, we can have Jesus at the center of our conversations but miss what Jesus is about. It is so easy to go through the motions. It is easy to become good churchgoers but miss the whole point. I am so glad I serve in a church that has a mission and vision greater than itself. I'm glad that our mission is to "belong and become [locally] in order that we might have greater impact [globally]." We really do exist for those outside the church. The members and attenders of our church are committed to being constantly reminded that church is not about us, and it's a thing of beauty to see the bride of Christ operate in such a selfless way.

- *Serve others who can't help themselves.*

You don't have to go very far to find someone who needs your help. There are probably older people living on your street who have leaky faucets, leaf-filled gutters, or shorted-out electrical sockets. At the grocery store you will almost certainly find a single mother worried about the price of baby formula because her job isn't paying enough for her to buy the type her child needs. If you're going to a ball game, you could very well run into the Miracle League or a similar organization that provides sporting opportunities for the mentally and physically challenged. When you're at the hospital visiting a friend or relative, stop by the children's wing, where you might find that 30 to 40 percent of patients are struggling with cancer. And it's more than likely that their parents are struggling in their own ways.

We have more than we need as Americans. Start somewhere—anywhere—and give of what you have to help someone else. You'll find that the more of yourself you give away, your resources as well as your time and energy, the more you find you didn't need all that excess in the first place. There are innumerable opportunities in this world to live and love like Jesus, and there are more needs than you could ever meet by yourself; but start somewhere, and encourage others to do likewise.

- *Live on less this year than you did last year.*

When Tami and I moved to Atlanta several years ago, we purchased the smallest house we could find in order to afford the mortgage payment, and it was still twice as much house as we had as young church planters. I still remember the first time someone moved out of our neighborhood and into a larger home a few subdivisions down the road. I didn't understand the concept of upsizing at that time, but it didn't take long for me to learn it. Before long, I found that I had become discontented with what I had, and it was easy to begin dreaming of something more, something bigger.

Somewhere between having teenagers and paying college tuition, I've learned that I don't need as much extra stuff as I used to, nor do I want as much as I used to want. Certainly, that's not to say I don't have wants. I do, but the freedom that comes from not constantly needing or wanting more is worth more than excess stuff. What if you set out to live on less this year than you did last year? What if you gave the excess away as a tangible representation of the freedom that comes with clearing out the junk in your life?

Imagine what we might ultimately accomplish for God's kingdom if we focused on having less, doing less, being less, getting less, and spending less. Perhaps, by operating with less, the result would, in fact, be more: more people living like Jesus, loving like Jesus, and leaving what Jesus left behind.

- *Giving breaks the greed in our lives.*

This may sound surprising coming from a pastor, but I hate giving campaigns of any kind. You can probably relate. However, lately I am beginning to see how significant they are, and not only for the good of what is being given to. Truthfully, I'm beginning to understand that one reason I hate them is that I really like hanging on to my money and my stuff for my own use. I want to spend on things I want, things I (think I) need; after all, I've worked really hard for them, and I think I deserve them.

We recently launched a new initiative at Mountain Lake Church in which I found myself laying it on the line like never before with respect to financial giving, and I wasn't the only one. Hundreds of people in our church community allowed themselves to go through a refining process that gave us all a different perspective. Rather than considering how much we could give up to accomplish God's work through our church, we gave in ways that reminded us that we are merely stewards, returning to God what has been His all along. We gave because we believe in the mission of creating a place where our friends and neighbors can belong in community with Christ followers. I gave because I know that my gifts, along with those of the many others who sacrificed, are going to make a difference and because I know I am going to spend the rest of my life living out the purposes behind these gifts.

Something happened to me during this last initiative that was different from other giving campaigns: I was released from the grip of stuff that had taken hold of me. God is doing a great work in me by loosening the grip of consumerism and materialism on my life, and even though I'm not cured yet, I'm getting better. I'm living for more of what Jesus lived for, and through that I'm learning to love more as Jesus loved.

Getting It

Jim came to me one day after attending a weekend service and said, "God has given me a vision to make Him the CEO of my company." I asked him what that meant, and Jim, who was a new follower of Jesus, said, "I am going to practice godly principles in my business, and I am going to make God the highest-paid employee in my company. It seems to me, if He is the CEO, He should be the highest-paid employee." He handed me a check for one hundred dollars and said, "Here is His first paycheck. I know it isn't much, but I've got to get there. This represents a start." Over the next few months, Jim came into my office every Monday with God's paycheck. One day after handing me a check, he told me he was going to begin giving God a ten-dollar raise each week, in order to more quickly reach his goal of making God the highest-paid employee in his company. As time would have it, Jim and I went different directions. I moved on to another city and a different ministry, but the last time I sat down with Jim, he explained that he had finally reached his goal.

Jim got it—Jesus was definitely in every part of Jim's life. He found a way to make God the CEO of not only his business but his life, his family, and his church. Life is certainly not all about money, but when we struggle with consumerism, it is an indication of where our heart is. When we begin to let go of all the things that find their ways into our lives as substitutes, we can begin to make Jesus the very center of our lives. As Jesus put it, "For where your treasure is, there your heart will be also" (Matt. 6:21).

||||||||||||||||||||||||||||||||||||||||||||||||||||||||||||||||||||||||||||||||||||

Missional Snapshot

Autumn Ward *is a stay-at-home mom who uses her passion to connect with the disconnected and uses her writing skills to develop children's curriculum.*

When I moved with my husband to plant a church in Cumming, Georgia, I was very much on mission to reach the people who were disconnected from Christ and the church. It was then that an opportunity to do writing with a nationally known Christian organization came my way. Before long, one assignment turned into another, which turned into speaking engagements, which turned into more writing. I was earning more money and more pats on the back. It was great . . . until I realized my focus had changed. I had become more concerned about my next writing assignment and how I could improve my life with my next paycheck than I was with the disconnected in my community. I was miserable.

When I figured out the stuff I bought with my money wasn't it, I decided to give every cent of the money I was making to the church. Did that help? Nope. It wasn't long after that, that God pulled me close and let me know it wasn't the money He wanted—He wanted me.

I was too tired and distracted to notice the checkout girl at the grocery store or the soccer coach, the guy changing my oil or the teachers at my children's school.

I knew I had done the right thing the moment I turned in my resignation. It took several weeks to refocus myself. I knew things had come full circle when I invited my pest control guy and a guy who cuts grass in our neighborhood to church in the same week. It felt great to care once again as they told me their stories. Is there a price? Everything has a price. Yes, the money for home projects and a better car is gone. But in the end, those things will fade. The mission of Jesus is the only thing that will last.

||||||||||||||||||||||||||||||||||||||||||||||||||||||||||||||||||||||||||||||||||||||

Something to Think About

1. When it comes to the church, are you more concerned with going to church or being the church? What is the difference between the two?

2. Describe how you can concentrate more on being the church as you follow Jesus.

3. If your treasure is an indication of where your heart is, what does it tell you about yourself?

4. When it comes to your life, would you describe Jesus as in or out? What about your church?

5. What are your next steps in making your life more about Jesus and less about you?

"Give to Caesar what is Caesar's and to God what is God's."
—MATTHEW 22:21

What Does a Missional Follower Look Like When It Comes to Politics?

I have been guilty of voting a straight ticket. I hate to admit it, but I did at one time walk into the voting booth and pull the lever without thinking. I did it only once. Maybe it was because I was too busy to keep informed or perhaps because I was lazy, or maybe I had read one of the voting guides designed to tell us how a good Christian votes. Whatever my reasoning, I hope you (and God) will forgive me for being naive, lazy, and narrow and for parking my brain, heart, and freedoms at the door of a voting booth.

Today, I have repented. I am rethinking my politics, including the issues, parties, and candidates that drive them. I'm no longer taking my freedom to vote for granted, and I refuse to sell out to a party that does all my thinking for me. I refuse to blindly adhere to any reading guide or anyone else's dogma without investigating it for myself through the lens of Jesus.

Unfulfilled Expectations

Unfortunately, the issue is much deeper than simply becoming more informed and voting our convictions. Our politics and attitudes about our politics have become a huge barrier to our missional engagement in the world. It was our hope that our political actions, at the end of the past century and the beginning of this century, would do much to right our nation morally and put us on the straight and narrow as a nation. We envisioned a better world, but, for better or worse, what many of us envisioned hasn't happened. The alliance of religion and Beltway politics has proved not to be the answer. Organizations like the Moral Majority and the Christian Coalition have had their moments in the political spotlight, only to ease off the stage of American politics without as much as an encore. We have had a conservative Christian president and a conservative Congress working hand in hand for the first time in many years under the backdrop of a conservative judicial branch, yet we have seen limited progress.

However, I don't want to be too hard on those who have fought hard for the soul of our nation. Who knows where we would be without those who have courageously laid it all on the line? We can't deny that there has been a saltlike effect in preserving the moral fabric of our nation. At the same time, if we have any notion that the answer to the moral and social issues of our day is a political surge by a conservative brand of Christianity, we will be greatly disappointed.

Generational Backlash

At the turn of this millennium, I don't think we expected the kind of backlash that we have experienced as a church. In *unChristian,* David Kinnaman and Gabe Lyons quoted one young Mississippian who, I'm afraid, describes the attitude of many people outside the church: "Christianity has become bloated with blind followers who would rather repeat slogans than actually feel true compassion and care. Christianity has become marketed and streamlined into a juggernaut of fear-mongering that has lost its own heart."[9] Unfortunately, our politics don't escape this sentiment. Using hard data, the authors found that "three-quarters of young outsiders and half of young churchgoers described present-day Christianity as 'too involved in politics.' Nearly two-thirds of [16- to 29-year-old] outsiders and nearly half of young born-again Christians said they perceived 'the political efforts of conservative Christians' to be a problem facing America."[10]

This places a burden on us as followers of Jesus. Have we in our attempt to save the soul of America lost an entire generation? This is a question worth pondering as missional followers of Jesus.

Land of the Free

Let me go on the record saying that I believe we live in the greatest country in the world. I love being an American. My son is fighting the war on terror. My grandfather was a naval machine gunner during World War II. He was there on D-day, fighting in the Battle of Normandy. I respect and appreciate many of the godly leaders we have in Washington, D.C., and I am indebted to many pastors and Christian activists who have made a difference in our country. However, I believe that being "wise as serpents and gentle as doves" is in order here.

In studying the Gospels, I am amazed at how nonpolitical Jesus was. It wasn't that He was against politics or, as far as that goes, for politics. He simply gave no indication that He felt politics had any significant impact on the kingdom of heaven. Once, when His religious opponents tried to draw Him in, His response was amazingly simple. They asked Jesus, "'Is it right to pay taxes to Caesar or not?' But Jesus, knowing their evil intent said, 'You hypocrites, why are you trying to trap me? Show me the coin used for paying the tax.' They brought him a denarius, and he asked them, 'Whose portrait is this? And whose inscription?' 'Caesar's,' they replied. Then he said to them, 'Give to Caesar what is Caesar's, and to God what is God's'" (Matt. 22:17b–21).

At first I find this dialogue surprising, but when we examine what it means to live and love like Jesus, we are introduced to a whole new way of thinking about politics. The way of Jesus transcends both the Right and the Left and brings us together, uniting us under common causes.

Two Converging Issues and Opportunities

I see two converging issues for followers of Jesus to address if we are to emulate His life with respect to our government affairs: our image and our syncretism of politics and Christianity. I've talked about our political image among younger generations, but I don't think our image problem stops there. When you consider the robust dialogue that occurs about Christians during major elections, it becomes obvious that our image issues go beyond our young and ideal, extending to a fairly wide-ranging demographic of Americans.

The Pew Research Center recently confirmed this in a study called "Mixed Trends in Religious Tolerance," in which they claimed that "Catholics and Jews, for example, once the objects of widespread and often institutionalized discrimination, are now viewed favorably by a sizable majority of Americans. But . . . evangelical Christians and especially Muslims are not fully accepted by many Americans."[11] If you are like me, I am a little (or a lot) surprised that evangelical Christians are lumped in with Muslims. I don't think it's fair, nor do I agree, but I'm simply reporting the facts. If anything, it indicates that our image problem runs deeper than with only emerging generations. When it comes to the issue of image, we as followers of Jesus have our work cut out for us.

This leads me to the second of the two issues facing the church: the syncretism of politics and Christianity. Christianity has always existed and even thrived within the context of opposition and oppression. The early church is a prime example: While it thrived in the early days in Jerusalem, it found a new gear in the context of persecution. "On that day a great persecution broke out against the church at Jerusalem, and all except the apostles were scattered throughout Judea and Samaria. . . . Those who had been scattered preached the word wherever they went" (Acts 8:1b, 4). We see the same kind of explosive movement today among the church in eastern Asia, which over the past fifty years has experienced rapid multiplication and growing influence among the people as it has been forced underground. There are early indications that the same type of movement is taking place in many Middle Eastern countries where Christianity is either illegal or disdained.

I once heard someone suggest that "when everybody's Christian, then nobody's Christian." Cultures that become "Christianized" seem to lose their steam. When Constantine declared Christianity the religion of the Roman Empire, on the surface it appeared to be a great victory. However, what followed was a watering down of what it meant to be a follower of Jesus and a converging of the secular with the sacred. Many of our practices in the church today have less to do with Jesus and more to do with the blending of the two at the hands of Constantine.

Even though the majority of Americans believe in a theistic God, that the Bible is the Word of God, that Jesus was God's Son, and that good people go to heaven and bad people go to hell, these beliefs don't make us a Christian nation any more than attending church, living in a red state, and being pro-life make a person a follower of Jesus. Becoming missional followers of Jesus puts us in stark contrast with liberals and conservatives. Jesus has a way of holding both ends in tension as He shows us a new way, the way of love.

Both issues present us with challenges and, at the same time, with incredible opportunities. We can change the way people think about the church and the way they think about Jesus by responding to the moral, social, and political issues of our world in the same manner that Jesus did when He lived on earth. Jesus's entire ministry was lived in the context of His kingdom, which was about bringing the rule of God into every sphere of life. We see this in one of His first trips to the synagogue in which He said, "The Spirit of the Lord is on me, because he has anointed me to preach good news to the poor. He has sent me to proclaim freedom for the prisoners and recovery of sight for the blind, to release the oppressed, to proclaim the year of the Lord's favor" (Luke 4:18–19). Even if we focused our efforts solely on the poor, the imprisoned, the blind, and the oppressed, not only would we overcome the image barrier, we would greatly enhance the mission of the church, making a difference in the areas Jesus cared about most.

As Jesus explained in His Sermon on the Mount, "You are the light of the world. A city on a hill cannot be hidden. . . . In the same way, let your light shine before men, that they may see your good deeds and praise your Father in heaven" (Matt. 5:14, 16). Imagine a world where followers of Jesus roll up their sleeves and work hand in hand with nonbelievers to make our world a better place. Imagine working to right many of the injustices of our world, not caring who gets the credit. I can't help but imagine that barriers would be lowered and a whole new image would emerge.

The good news is that this is already happening among many followers of Jesus. In an article in *USA Today* titled "Christian Right's Alliances Bend Political Spectrum," Susan Page reported, "In recent years, without much notice, conservative Christians also have helped force the State Department to place a higher priority on battling religious persecution, set the stage for a cease-fire in Sudan, enact legislation aimed at reducing prison rape in the USA, and push for more funds to fight AIDS in Africa. In the process, they have forged coalitions with—or sometimes simply pulled in the same direction as—activists who more often are their adversaries."[12]

This is good news for us followers of Jesus who are working to change our image and bring down barriers that would hinder us from living and loving like Jesus and leaving what Jesus left behind.

Bottom Line

As we live like Jesus, love like Jesus, and leave what Jesus left behind (those who live and love like Jesus), we must ask, "What does Jesus care about?" and leverage any opportunity to see His kingdom come on earth as it is in heaven, no matter what side of the aisle it puts us on.

To be on God's side is to be reminded of the underprivileged. It challenges our attitude and our politics that always neglect the poor, the vulnerable, the helpless. The Jesus way challenges our self-interest and casts a spotlight on the whole of the earth and all that is in it. The Jesus way confronts us with our own tendency to consume all of the earth's natural resources and compels us to consider our responsibility to care for the whole of the earth. The Jesus way forces us to struggle with what it means to be peacemakers on this earth and to reconsider those whom the destructive nature of war has left behind. The Jesus way not only challenges us to consider the rights of those unborn but to take action in providing a better world for those who already live. The Jesus way challenges us to reconsider our tendency to stand on the Right or Left when it comes to politics and to offer a new vision of faith, hope, and love.[13]

It is our responsibility as missional followers of Jesus to challenge and inform political parties based on the teachings of the gospel and the coming of His kingdom. Living like Jesus relates to the things that we are most compelled to inform and challenge. Loving like Jesus relates to how we approach the Left, Right, and everything in the middle. Leaving what Jesus left behind relates to our responsibility to leave behind a world better than we found it.

||||||||||||||||||||||||||||||||||||||||||||||||||||||||||||||||||||||||||||||||||||||

Missional Snapshot

Sarah Anderson *is a writer and editor for student-based curriculum and is the daughter of a former Republican presidential candidate.*

I grew up outside the electrically charged bubble of Washington and have witnessed individuals from all political parties claim their allegiance to organized Christianity and devotion to God, only to quickly and efficiently disappoint. I am reminded that no elected official, no party, is single-handedly going to usher in the kingdom of God.

As a politically conscious person, and as a part of a politically savvy family, I have wrestled with what this requires of me, a follower of Jesus first, a patriot second. Marrying politics and Christ requires being a more critical thinker, in pursuit of Jesus's way ahead of the "American" way. It means broadening perspective, from election year to eternity. It means practicing righteous positions, not necessarily right parties. This shift of thinking requires increased responsibility. Nearly anyone can fight hard enough to win, but in the process am I reflecting Jesus?

My entire family remains actively involved in the D.C. political scene at various levels, with the exception of me, a three-year resident of Atlanta. Together, we pursue Christ, no matter what the avenue, regardless of location, title, or station of life. Our passion is the path of Jesus, above all. We know that the right people, funding, and beliefs will not be the catalysts for transformation. We will be. Not because of status, influence, or public approval but because we are courting Christ. Collectively, whether inside or apart from the political pandemonium that can be Washington, we will be the ones to usher in the grassroots way of Jesus, and we will do so as Christ followers, regardless of the ruling party in the White House, the Congress, or the Supreme Court.

||||||||||||||||||||||||||||||||||||||||||||||||||||||||||||||||||||||||||||||||||||||

Something to Think About

1. Why is it important to be informed about politics?
2. When you vote, does it reflect the way of Jesus or the religious culture? Why?

3. When it comes to social injustices of our world, what are our responsibilities?

4. Do you think America is a Christian nation? Why or why not?

5. Why do you think Jesus had little to say about politics and government?

> *"Look at the birds of the air; they do not sow or reap*
> *or store away in barns, and yet your heavenly Father feeds them.*
> *Are you not much more valuable than they?"*
> —MATTHEW 6:26

What Does a Missional Follower Look Like in the Green Space?

I recently returned home from a weeklong vacation in one of the most beautiful places in the world, Florida's gulf shores. I have stood at the edge of the Mediterranean Sea, I've sailed in the Caribbean, and I've watched the gigantic waves break on the sand of the north shore of Oahu, but nothing surpasses the beauty of the crystal white sands and blue waters of the gulf shores. My stay in a condo was a gift for a week of re-creation in my own life. Each morning I would wake up at six o'clock, drawn to the deck that rose up over the white dunes, giving me a unique vantage point where I enjoyed my coffee and a time of quiet reflection. Regardless of whether it was early morning or late night, the crashing of the waves against the sandy shores brought my soul to life again. Having spent a week in this marvel of creation, I can understand why God saw that His work was good when He completed the third day of Creation, which included the oceans and seas. There is something about water that speaks of God's calming nature. It was good!

All Things Green and More

Like any vacation, of course, all good things have to come to an end. But the next morning at home, I found myself in another piece of paradise: the patio behind my house. When we first moved in, it was a typical suburban house, the three-quarter-acre lot having been stripped of anything remotely green by the developer. For the first couple of years, the only way to enjoy our backyard was to go out the front door and around the outside of the house. It wasn't very inviting. Like most suburbanites, we drove into our garages at the end of the day and settled into the quiet tranquility of our kitchen and living room after the garage doors closed behind us.

Over the past few years, however, Tami and I have created an environmental refuge in our backyard. During a remodeling project, I decided to remove a window that faced the rear of the house and replace it with a door. The door was a powerful thing that provided access to a whole new world; soon I began to dream about what could be in my backyard. As my dreams gave way to a vision, the yard was transformed by a patio, an old swing, and a small pond complete with a waterfall. The surrounding landscaping includes river birches, azaleas, lilies, gardenias, cypress trees, and an assortment of colorful annuals. Our little garden has become the habitat for a family of frogs and an assortment of butterflies, not to mention the cardinals, finches, blue jays, and hummingbirds that all call our garden home. The choir of frogs, birds, and crickets—all singing to the background of the trickling water flowing from our waterfall—is indeed sweet music to my ears.

I have had countless encounters with God there as I've listened to the sounds of nature. I've had my best conversations with my wife and kids in this garden. I celebrated twenty-five years of marriage with my wife on a candlelit night in that sacred spot. It has become a place where I recenter on my life and relationships, and

I love to share the space with my friends. When I sit in my spot, listening to the animals and dreaming, I thank God for my chance to enjoy His creation.

God the Creator

As I sit in my garden and reflect on its beauty and my role in developing it, I can't help but relate to God our Creator. I feel closer to Him, as I am His child, sharing His bent to create and to nurture. I look around at our little garden and delight in His goodness. As I read about His Creation in Genesis 1, I see it through a different light. I can only imagine the sense of accomplishment He felt when He reflected at the end of the day, seeing that it was good. With each passing day, as God created the earth, He took something that was formless and barren and created a masterpiece. For six days He created. He began with the creation of light that separated from darkness, and then, out of an expanse of water, He created land. This was followed by the creation of an ecosystem that was divided by seasons and gave host to all living vegetation. From there God filled the oceans with all manner of sea life and the dry land with all kinds of living creatures.

Yet in all the glory of the natural creation, God saw that it was not complete. So on the sixth day He created mankind. With this creation we read, "God saw all that He had made, and it was very good" (Gen. 1:31a). Did you notice that? Very good. Here the story takes a different twist. Man wasn't simply created to be a part of creation, but man was created to care for all of creation. God created the earth and everything in it and gave it to man. What a gift! What an amazing responsibility! Talk about being given the family business!

Then God said, "Let us make man in our image, in our likeness, and let them rule over the fish of the sea and the birds of the air, over the livestock, over all the earth,

and over all the creatures that move along the ground."
. . . "Rule over the fish of the sea and the birds of the air
and over every living creature that moves on the ground."
Then God said, "I give you every seed-bearing plant on
the face of the whole earth and every tree that has fruit
with seed in it. They will be yours for food. And to all the
beasts of the earth and all the birds of the air and all the
creatures that move on the ground—everything that has
the breath of life in it—I give every green plant for food."
And it was so. God saw all that he had made, and it was
very good. (Gen. 1:26, 28b–31a)

Think about it: God wonderfully created the entire earth and
gave it to us as a gift to care for, preserve, enjoy, and share. Certainly
God could have made the earth self-sustaining. After all, it was perfect and without sin. Yet God chose to create us in such a way and
place us right in the middle with the wonderful responsibility to be
its caretakers. When we reflect on this, it is hard to believe we are
often so careless with it.

When it comes to caring for the environment, however, I confess that I have been a habitual violator. I have sinned against the
environment because, like most Americans, I am a consumer by
nature. Therefore, when it comes to rethinking what it means to be
a missional follower of Jesus, I must spend time reflecting on the
stewardship of our environment or, in this case, the lack of stewardship of our environment. Why have we been so negligent? As
followers of Jesus, why have we not led the charge in preserving the
environment God created for us?

Enlarging Our Vision

I serve in a church in one of the most beautiful areas of the
Southeast. We are located north of Atlanta, in the foothills of the
mountains and to the west of a beautiful lake. We have four seasons,

and each one brings its share of breathless moments. Within thirty minutes, I can either be hiking the Appalachian Trail or pulled behind a boat in an inner tube. Our church is situated on a thirty-two-acre campus that is mostly undeveloped. A creek divides our property, with the land to the front of the creek representing most of the developable land and the area to the rear undeveloped forest. Recently, we hired a design firm to help us create a master site plan for our campus that will incorporate the entire thirty-two acres. This was our third shot at a master site plan; each time previously we had walked away feeling that somehow we didn't get the full impact of what God wants to do with our campus.

Thanks to a firm that thinks outside the box, our vision is expanding. This design team has helped us look at our campus through the lens of our Creator God, expanding our vision beyond parking places and seats to how we can help people connect with God and all of His creation through our structure. What was once a necessary building construction project has now become an opportunity to create something on this wonderful canvas that God has entrusted us with. It is an exciting and incredible challenge.

As individuals we must begin to see our little part of the world as the master site plan of God, a canvas He has entrusted to us. Imagine if we looked at our lawns, gardens, flower boxes, and every other little patch as an opportunity to care for creation. Beyond that, we must view our responsibility as a collaborative one, committed to the common good in our communities, states, and world. This responsibility is nothing short of a Great Commission that begins right here at home and takes us to the ends of the earth.

Fear of Appearing Too (gasp!) Liberal

I think many of us have a tendency to avoid anything that lines up on the Left side of political issues as if it were a kind of disease. We stay away from issues like the environment, social justice, AIDS, and civil rights, leaving them for the blue-state thinkers. How is that possible when the One we are following is the chief advocate in these crises? We as missional followers of Jesus have failed to address many issues in our world because of this tendency to avoid association with those who have opposing viewpoints. Do we not trust our convictions? Do we not believe in the actions of Jesus when He cared for the sick and the needy? We can learn from many different perspectives, and when it comes to Jesus, He refuses to be put in a box of conservatism versus liberalism. God is the Creator, and He has given us His creation as a gift with a direct imperative to care for it. It is our responsibility. Anything short of that is sin.

Becoming a missional follower of Jesus leads us to new relationships and forms of collaboration. Following the way of Jesus puts our stewardship and calling to take care of God's creation above our reputation and beyond our petty differences.

An Abundance Mentality

Could it be that living in America, where everything we need is in gross abundance, has conditioned us to think that nature is an endless supply of resources? Often we live as if we are at the center of creation, as if everything that exists, exists for us. While there is no doubt that God values people more than anything else in creation, we must also consider that the earth is a gift, without which we have no home. When God created us and placed us in the garden with the imperative to care for it, I don't believe He had anything else in mind. He didn't put us in the garden and say, "Get rich from it."

God created a planet with resources to provide for the needs of everyone on it. I believe He knew that some areas of the earth would need help from others, but in the name of brotherhood we would be citizens of the globe, a family that cared about the needs of one another as well as future generations. We don't have a resource problem on the earth (with some people starving and some getting fat); we have an allocation problem. There is enough food and water for everyone on the globe, but maybe we Americans are monopolizing it.

Creation Recenters Our Lives

Reviewing Genesis and the story of Creation, we see an amazing and enlightening pattern emerging that consisted of reflection and rest: "God saw all that He had made, and it was very good. . . . By the seventh day God had finished the work He had been doing; so on the seventh day He rested from all His work" (Gen. 1:31a, 2:2).

When we create green spaces within our lives or take time to enjoy the green that already exists, they become places where we can reflect and rest. They often represent places where we become accustomed to hearing God. God invites us into His creation to recenter our lives. The times I feel most alive and closest to God are the times when I withdraw into His creation. I can truthfully say that God has brought the most healing and renewal to my life in times when He has moved me out of my routine of busyness into His creation.

I recall a fifteen-mile hike with my son on the Appalachian Trail during a time we both needed to recenter. We spent the first part of our journey getting to know each other again. By the middle of our journey, we had become reacquainted with God and His wonderful creation; and by the end of our journey, we came face-to-face with who we were and our greatest struggles. When we left the mountain that day, we left behind much of what we didn't need. We had failed to realize how our own busyness and pursuit of everything temporal had numbed us to the relationships that really matter. On the mountain, we left the stress of our lives and exchanged it for a whole new sense of liveliness. Our senses intensified. We became more aware of ourselves and each other. At some point along the way, we ceased to talk and we really started listening. We discovered once again that all we need is Jesus and each other.

It is in God's creation that we rest and meet ourselves. Perhaps the anxiety we feel as we slow down and rest is a symptom of the addiction we have to the adrenaline rush of our roller-coaster lives. Or perhaps we have an inflated sense of ourselves and our contribution to our world that keeps us from stopping and enjoying creation. Go ahead and get up right now. Put down this book and take a walk in nature, or sit by a lake and reflect on God. Spend a Sabbath in nature, remembering that it was on the very first Sabbath, when God had completed His work, that He reflected and marveled at His creation. He was overwhelmed by its goodness, and, after He saw that it was very good, He rested. He set aside a day to reflect, rest, renew, restore, rethink, recalculate, and recalibrate.

Creation Declares His Glory

One summer, when my kids were young teenagers, I spent a month working with pastors, church planters, and missionaries throughout the western United States. I decided to take the family with me and spend a few days sightseeing. I had seen many pictures and heard people speak about the rare beauty of the West, but I had not experienced it for myself. We began and ended our trip in Albuquerque, New Mexico, but not before we had driven through the Black Canyon of Colorado and the rugged terrain of Utah, marveled at the rock formations in the Arches National Park, watched the sun rise over the Grand Canyon, marveled at the Petrified Forest, and reflected on the various hues in the Painted Desert. I had no idea of the kind of beauty we would see, and we were awestruck by God's creation.

While traveling out West, I kept getting this sense of "otherness." I have always known and fully embraced God as the Creator and Sustainer of all things, but there was an additional dimension about His creation that I became aware of during that trip. Viewing a part of creation that I wasn't accustomed to made me really begin to see how important God's creation is in revealing Himself to us. It made sense to me why the West, or at least certain parts of it, had become the mecca of New Age spirituality. God's creation clearly demands some kind of explanation and exhortation, so it made sense to me that no matter where we went we found evidence of man worshiping a higher power. God's creation declares His glory even before we know the name of God. It also makes sense that those of us who worship the God of creation should be the first in line to care for it. When we are not, our inconsistency creates confusion for others.

Jesus and Nature

Jesus obviously lived in the midst of and loved nature, as many of His greatest truths arose from simple examples from the environment around Him. He taught His most significant message about the kingdom of God out in the open, from a mountaintop. As He taught, He drew examples from the birds fluttering nearby and the lilies growing radiantly in the field. He expressed the care of God for His people by saying, "If that is how God clothes the grass of the field, which is here today and tomorrow is thrown into the fire, will he not much more clothe you, O you of little faith?" (Matt. 6:30).

When He faced His greatest challenge and toughest struggle, Jesus retreated to the garden to pray. There He met God in the quiet and solitude of nature, finding resolve for the task. It was there He surrendered His life and became determined to make His greatest sacrifice. He came face-to-face with His mortality, gaining strength for those final moments, being reminded of why He had come, and renewing His love for us. There He prayed for us (John 17:20–26).

In looking at the life of Jesus, I am challenged to hear God speak to me from nature. As I look at the birds that have made my garden their sanctuary, I am reminded that God is my sanctuary. When I see how Jesus withdrew to nature, I'm reminded of how the stillness and solitude of nature is where I can best see and hear God. I'm reminded that the answers I seek most are not far away.

Taking Care of Creation

When it comes to our environment, it does seem that many of us have lost our way, forgetting our role in creation care. What is our responsibility? How do we find our way back? Here are ways to begin.

Read Up

The first step toward finding our way in creation care is getting informed. Groups like Target Earth bring together the whole idea of being missional by caring for the earth and the poor. As stated on its Web site, www.targetearth.org, "The mission of Target Earth is 'Serving the Earth, Serving the Poor.' We focus on those regions of the world that are most devastated by the mix of human suffering and the destruction of the earth where people live on a dollar a day or less."

While the care of nature is certainly not restricted to followers of Jesus, nor is it even dominated by them, many are blazing a new trail when it comes to caring for our environment. There are pioneers like Tri Robinson, pastor of Vineyard Church in Boise, Idaho, who is connecting the dots between our mission and our environment. In his book *Saving God's Green Earth,* Robinson talked about his own migration toward the environment: "I was always afraid to use the word 'environment' because I didn't want to be labeled a liberal. In the political landscape of the United States, environmentalism has always connected with a liberal perspective on the world. If you were a liberal, you were also supposedly for many other things that I simply could not accept or attach myself to. And while I shared many of the ideals of 'conservatives,' I viewed the environment as one issue that I could let slide. But that began to change when I realized I couldn't let political affiliation dissuade my higher allegiance to God's kingdom, and from my charge as a Christian to be a good steward of all God's creation."[14]

For most of us, there is much we can learn from people like Robinson who are leading the Jesus way as it relates to our environment. Don't limit yourself to the perspective of Christians in this arena—there are countless other resources available on practical care of the environment.

Use Only What You Need

I have a friend who eats until he is almost full and heats his house until he is almost comfortable. As a matter of fact, he does everything "almost." With the exception of following Jesus, in which he is all-out.

However, on the whole, when it comes down to the world's standards, we are spoiled gluttons. We consume the majority of the world's resources. If you are like me, it is a lifestyle. Reduce the amount of resources you use by carpooling to church with people in your neighborhood. When you prepare a meal, cook only what you'll eat and be careful not to let leftovers rot in the refrigerator for weeks. Turn on only the lights in the rooms you're occupying. Reduce your consumption of electricity by turning your thermostat up a few degrees (or down, depending on the season). You might be astounded at the difference it makes in your electric bill and how little you notice the change in comfort. Take on a minimal way of life and consume only what you need.

Start Recycling and Reduce Your Trash

There are two things we all can do when it comes to recycling. First, buy products that are healthy for the environment and that are biodegradable. Second, recycle your garbage. All it requires is a little research for services in your area that collect recycle waste and three containers: one for paper, one for plastics, and one for aluminum. Also, look for alternative ways of consuming—instead of killing tons of trees and stacking piles of newspapers and magazines around the house, read the periodicals online. Most of us have tons of grocery bags we can reuse on our frequent trips to the market.

Look for Energy-saving Alternatives

Often we choose the products we use based on efficiencies that result in cost savings. For example, I bought my large pickup truck when gas sold for $1.50 a gallon. Today, I am paying nearly $3.00 a gallon for the same gas, and my truck is no longer affordable. I based my most recent auto purchase solely on its cost. If possible, change the way you make family purchases to reflect what is best for the environment. There are all kinds of simple, energy-saving alternatives—from automobiles to lightbulbs—that over the long haul can make a significant difference in our environment.

Take on a Conservation Project

Clean up the earth with a group from your church. Join an organization devoted to saving a species. Create a green space on a vacant lot. Adopt a city park that needs care. Make it a habit to bend over and pick up a piece of trash. Partner with a group of local environmentalists. The need is great, and you won't have to search long to find a group that's doing something you're passionate about.

As missional followers of Jesus, we reflect the heart of God when we are actively engaged in environmental issues. Caring for our environment ensures that not only can we enjoy and recenter in our environment; our future generations will be able to as well. Being involved in our environment would not only redeem our reputation but our planet as well.

||||||||||||||||||||||||||||||||||||||||||||||||||||||||||||||||||||||||||||||||||

Missional Snapshot

Bob Bergmen *is an architect and part of the design team for Visioneering Studios specializing in architectural evangelism.*

As an architectural firm our assignment was to design the expansion of a church on the Front Range of the Rocky Mountains. After a couple of days of snooping around and camping out on the site, we gained surprising insights. Three "people groups" were not attending the church. We noticed that the "tree-huggers," "highland farmers," and "techies" were missing on campus. The church body and these three groups all enjoyed dramatic views of fourteen of the fourteen-thousand-foot peaks of the Rocky Mountains. On the first day our camera captured inspiring watercolors frame by frame as the sun set behind the range. These observations led to a design that made use of native grasses and natural trails connecting to the nearby community. The new buildings on campus were positioned to take full advantage of the views while at the same time creating multilevel courtyards for all groups to connect with one another as well as with God.

Architect Renzo Piano once said, "My profession, as an architect is to create places for people. Places are where experiences meet and differences disappear." In summary, our design approach was to attract neighbors to a common ground where diverse people could meet in safety and be exposed to the Master of the universe. As architects we are called to reconnect others to our wonderful Creator and His creation.

||||||||||||||||||||||||||||||||||||||||||||||||||||||||||||||||||||||||||||||||||

Something to Think About

1. Reflect on a time and a place where you recentered your life in nature.

2. Why do you think God gave us dominion over everything He created on this earth?

3. What does it mean to be a good steward of the environment?

4. What simple steps do you take to care for the environment?

5. How can taking care of the environment lead to being a missional follower of Jesus?

"Greater love has no one than this,
that one lay down his life for his friends."
—JOHN 15:13

What Does a Missional Follower Look Like on the Battlefield?

I'm almost hesitant to write about the war on terror. I'm afraid that most of us who try to put in our two cents have no idea what we're talking about—many of us are simply quoting a party line. However, while I'm not claiming to be an authority on international politics, I do feel I have a different perspective from many others who speak on the subject. My son is a soldier, having served a fifteen-month tour in Afghanistan. So while I can't help but think that war is evil, it is also often necessary; and regardless of whether we think the cause is just, we find ourselves in the middle of it. I think it's important to point out that it's not only I who have something at stake—we all do. The war on terror is exactly what we call it: Global terrorism will bring fear into our lives and take our basic freedoms from us if it is not fought. I don't understand the evil and depravity behind it, but I do understand that we are all at risk.

Like many of us, this journey began for me on September 11, 2001, a day that I remember with uncanny clarity. I was in a conference room, leading my team in our monthly meeting. I began with a devotional, after which a knock came on our door, and we were alerted to the news that a plane had crashed into the World

Trade Center. I rushed out of the office to the nearby TV monitor in time to see the second plane destroy the second tower. Life that day and in the following days became surreal; the events caused us all to realize we were under an attack far worse than anyone could have imagined. By the end of the day, almost three thousand people had lost their lives, United 93 had been brought down by a heroic act over a field in Pennsylvania, the World Trade Center towers had crashed violently to the ground, and the Pentagon had been crushed on one side. Truly, this was the day that the modern world changed.

All the employees of our organization met in the chapel, where we wept openly and fell on our faces, crying out to God. Our first responders—chaplains and disaster relief leaders—began to mobilize, and before we said amen to our prayers, they were in their vehicles making their way to what became known as Ground Zero.

The day I made my first trip to Ground Zero is etched permanently in my mind. I took my then seventeen-year-old son, Dave, with me, and we saw the once imposing, majestic structure that had become nothing more than a twisted and broken pile of rubble, with smoke still rising from the top. There were people everywhere, and it was obvious many of them had lost someone very dear to them. Makeshift memorials were strewn all over the sidewalks and surrounding areas. The fire station that lost so many brave firefighters stood abandoned. For about four or five hours Dave and I walked around the ruins, barely speaking. Many times that day we broke down and wept. My son used his pen to articulate his deep pain, drawing it like a sword and etching his reflections on innumerable makeshift memorials. And even though our worlds would take two completely different directions in reconciling the emotional, intellectual, and spiritual turbulence unearthed in our lives that day, we have both been forever impacted and knitted together by the experience.

I now take fairly regular trips to the Middle East with brave and remarkable people from the church where I serve. We are on a mission of peace, with plans to care for people who are living in garbage dumps, to develop computer labs for churches in the slums, to tell people about Jesus's love when it's permissible, and always to share His love through our actions. We know that even as we are there sharing the message of Jesus, we will be at risk—some going before us have even died. A young boy who is hearing the message of jihad may choose the way of peace, but others may choose the way of terror. We walk the same streets they walk, compelled by Jesus's love to bring His message of hope and love to a people who may have never heard it before.

As I travel through the Middle East, I think of Dave. He serves in the U.S. Army as a reconnaissance scout with the 82nd Airborne, in one of the most challenging, dangerous, and difficult military occupational specialties in the armed forces. I never knew exactly where he was, what he was doing, or when I would hear from him; I knew only that he was usually along the Afghanistan/Pakistan border. He had very few comforts, and he lived in almost constant danger. I do know he spent most of his time hunting down the Taliban, sometimes for weeks at a time. He took three showers one month and was shot at more times than I want to think about. One day he was hit with an improvised explosive device (IED), and miraculously he walked away. But I know that others have been hit and didn't walk away.

When he told me he was going to enlist, the only thing I could say was, "I would rather you die for something than live for nothing." His humble reply was, "Yeah, that's what I was thinking." In another conversation he shared with me that he felt serving our country was his responsibility. I'm glad he realizes that to whom much is given, much is required. When I think of him, I am often drawn to the Scripture in which Jesus stated, "Greater love has no one than this, that one lay down his life for his friends" (John 15:13). Obviously, as I write this chapter, I long for his safe return, and my prayer is that as you opened this book you saw a dedication that reads something like, "To my beloved son, who has returned."

My son and I have taken two completely different paths, but I can't help believing that both of them are necessary. I wish there were no such things as evil, war, crime, pain, hurt, and sin in this world, but it's not the case. I wish that Jesus had not had to come and fight the ultimate battle for our peace, but He did!

If my son were not in uniform, I could see how easy it would be to get on the pacifist bandwagon that suggests we avoid war at any cost. For you who do, I understand. On the other hand, it's also as easy to get on the "just-war" bandwagon that suggests certain circumstances and situations justify a military response. But consider this in light of the fronts of the war that my story represents, mine and my son's: It is not simply my son's war, but it is mine as well. I can choose to bury my head in the sand, but ultimately people, like my son, are fighting the war for me. As Jesus said, "You will hear of wars and rumors of wars, but see to it that you are not alarmed. Such things must happen, but the end is still to come. Nation will rise against nation, and kingdom against kingdom" (Matt. 24:6–7a). I wish I had nothing at stake, but I do. You do too. It is our war if we care about the future of our freedom, our children's freedom, and our grandchildren's freedom. One thing is for sure: "Nation will rise against nation, and kingdom against kingdom." How would Jesus live and love with respect to the conflict we find ourselves in or the many we have yet to see?

Love the Whole World

It was easy for me to bury my head in the sand, ignoring the problem, until I had something deeply personal at stake. I was content to let other people wage the war with their words and actions. But as I considered my new role as the father of a soldier, I realized that as Jesus loves the world, I am called to do the same. Loving the world means loving people who are like us, but it also means loving people who are very different from us. Loving the world means loving people who are easy to love and loving people who are very difficult to love. Loving the world means loving those who love us, but it also means loving our enemies. And it's hard.

If we love the world, we are compelled to respond to the world's unrest. As we examine the life of Jesus, He was often seen responding with a special compassion for those who needed loving the most. One of the most significant ways we are to love the world is to spend time in it. We must go into all the world, even though it is easier, safer, and more convenient to stay home. I know that when I go to the Islamic world I run the risk of falling in love with the Muslim people and their culture. I might even love people I have no hope of converting to my faith. I run the risk of loving someone who could ultimately bring great harm to me.

It's this kind of love that turns our world upside down. If I love as Jesus loves, I can't help but go. My world gets really, really large. My agenda gets preempted. My bank account gets depleted. It is much easier to debate and debate and debate, but if we as followers of Jesus are committed to living, loving, and leaving like Jesus, lip service is no longer an option for us—we must actively love. We must go.

Be Informed

Did you know that ten school-age children were injured in west Afghanistan recently when a suicide bomber blew himself up in a busy city area? Did you know much of what is fueling the surge of violence in Afghanistan is the worldwide opium trade? Did you know that the Department of Defense has a Web site that is updated daily with the names of all of our soldiers who have paid the ultimate sacrifice? I often read through the names of those soldiers, and

I pray for their families. Sometimes they are my age, and I envision what their children must feel, and I pray for them. Other times they are really young, and I pray for their mothers and fathers, finding it frighteningly easy to empathize with them. Some days I discover that someone from the 82nd Airborne is listed, and I'm reminded that we made it another day without dreaded news. Still, at the same time I can't rejoice because I know other families received the notice.

I've been told by some to stop looking at that stuff, but I can't. There is simply too much at stake for me. Here is what I know regardless of my feelings or convictions about this war: I can become informed, and this information can compel me to action. If being a missional follower of Jesus is really about living like Jesus and loving like Jesus, then I can't help but respond to the many atrocities of this world.

Encourage Troops and Their Families

Tami and I experienced much love and concern after our son was deployed. It is a constant reminder that God really cares for me, my family, and especially my son. Each comment and prayer I receive is a personal message from God Himself, as I am reminded that His eye is on the sparrow. During my son's deployment, a lady stopped me and told me that she admired me. She said she knew it had to be hard having my son overseas in the middle of a war, but that she admired the fact that I was positive and encouraging about it. While I often struggle with fear and anxiety, I have run across many parents who struggle far more. These interactions serve as a great reminder to me that no matter what, I can trust God—I really do believe God is in control and that I can trust Him with the life of my son.

I like returning the love. As I walk down the international terminal of the airport, it is often filled with soldiers. I once noticed one with the Ranger insignia, and I approached him and learned he was leaving his family for Kuwait. As we talked about where he was going and what he did, I told him about my son because they shared a similar specialty. I thanked him and wished him the best.

At these and other times, I've seen firsthand what a conversation like this does for a young man facing the uncertainties of his first combat mission. I watched him grow taller as people approached him and thanked him for what he was doing. I watched his confidence grow as people promised to pray for him. I want to live a life that encourages soldiers and families of soldiers to trust God with their lives and the lives of their loved ones. Is this not what we see Jesus doing throughout His life and ministry? When He was confronted with the sacrifice of others, He recognized and affirmed it (see Matt. 11:7–15).

Pray for Peace and Protection

Jesus calls us to be peacemakers, even calling the peacemaker "blessed" (Matt. 5:9). I know He delights when we pray for peace, and I know He is delighted when we pray our Lord's Prayer: "your kingdom come, . . . on earth as it is in heaven" (Matt. 6:10). As you might imagine, I often find myself praying for peace and protection for my son, but lately I find my prayers growing broader. I pray for the protection of those troops serving in Afghanistan, Iraq, and the hundreds of other sites around the world where our troops are stationed. I find myself praying for the Muslims, both militant and peacekeeping. I pray for the countries harboring terrorists and for the countries fighting terrorism. I also pray for our churches—churches in my community, in America, and in the world. I pray that we might be harbingers of peace on earth and goodwill toward all men.

In addition, I have learned much from my son recently. I admire his service and his commitment, and thank God for making him the warrior Tami and I have prayed he would be. I see him having become a man beyond his years, and I see him learning what it means to be a follower of Jesus.

Be Salt and Light

We live in an imperfect world filled with sin, suffering, hurt, pain, war, murder, and lawlessness. It is our responsibility as missional followers of Jesus to bring His light and His love into this broken world. I'm thankful that I have the perspective in which to see this demonstrated in practical ways through our work in the Middle East: Our goal as a military in Afghanistan is not simply to remove the Taliban, but it also involves building a new infrastructure where peace and freedom can thrive. There are countless opportunities for the men and women in uniform to live like Jesus and love like Jesus, and they are fulfilling this call when schools are being opened and Muslim girls are able to attend for the first time in their lives, when religious freedoms are extended and spiritual choices are now theirs to make.

Yet there are thieves and murderers and terrorists in our world who strap explosives to their chests and walk into sidewalk cafés, detonating and killing themselves along with the innocent people around them. We desperately need salt and light in this war on terror. Salt and light allow us to hang on to our sanity and comfort our soldiers when they are defending freedom to the point of death. The Gospel of Matthew records Jesus's words: "Let your light shine before men, that they may see your good deeds and praise your Father in heaven" (5:16). The light shines even on the battlefield.

Gain Comfort from Scripture

Certainly, I don't like war. I don't know many people who do. In a conversation with my son, he admitted he couldn't wait to return home and put the war behind him. He longed for a simpler, more peaceful life—cruising our beautiful nation on his Harley Davidson. Not much for a kid who has seen it all and paid such a high price. Yet I know, as he does, that those who fight for our freedom often face the types of atrocities that are hard to leave behind, and he and I are both thankful for the comfort we draw from God's Word. Sadly, we know that war is part of living in a world where there is sin, and that as long as men hijack jets, fly them into buildings, and kill innocent people, war will be necessary. Solomon understood this when he wrote:

> To every thing there is a season, and a time to every pur-
> pose under the heaven:
> A time to be born, and a time to die; a time to plant, and
> a time to pluck up that which is planted;
> A time to kill, and a time to heal; a time to break down,
> and a time to build up;
> A time to weep, and a time to laugh; a time to mourn,
> and a time to dance;
> A time to cast away stones, and a time to gather stones
> together; a time to embrace, and a time to refrain
> from embracing;
> A time to get, and a time to lose; a time to keep, and a
> time to cast away;
> A time to rend, and a time to sew; a time to keep silence,
> and a time to speak;
> A time to love, and a time to hate; a time of war, and a
> time of peace. (Eccles. 3:1–8 KJV)

Accomplish Good during War

When my son left for the front lines, I had no idea that much of what our troops do is focused on humanitarian efforts. As Nehemiah rebuilt the walls of Jerusalem, our servicemen and women are rebuilding the walls of many nations. In Afghanistan children are returning to schools by the thousands, electricity is being restored, women are slowly regaining their rights and are gaining protection under the law, drugs are being eradicated, orphans are being cared for, and liberties and freedoms are being restored.

When we as missional followers of Jesus respond within our contexts as Jesus would respond—even in the midst of wars—with love, servanthood, and grace, peace can reign and hope can be restored. What we learn from the Gospels is there is only one uniform: that of a follower of Jesus.

A Personal Note

Shortly after my son deployed, I received an e-mail from my cousin with a prayer of safety for my son. She concluded by quoting Psalm 91, often referred to as the Soldier's Psalm:

He who dwells in the shelter of the Most High
    will rest in the shadow of the Almighty.
I will say of the LORD, "He is my refuge and my fortress,
    my God, in whom I trust."
Surely he will save you from the fowler's snare
    and from the deadly pestilence.
He will cover you with his feathers,
    and under his wings you will find refuge;
    his faithfulness will be your shield and rampart.
You will not fear the terror of night,
    nor the arrow that flies by day,
nor the pestilence that stalks in the darkness,
    nor the plague that destroys at midday.
A thousand may fall at your side,
    ten thousand at your right hand,
    but it will not come near you.
You will only observe with your eyes
    and see the punishment of the wicked.
If you make the Most High your dwelling—
    even the LORD, who is my refuge—
then no harm will befall you,
    no disaster will come near your tent.

> For he will command his angels concerning you
>> to guard you in all your ways;
> they will lift you up in their hands,
>> so that you will not strike your foot against a stone.
> You will tread upon the lion and the cobra;
>> you will trample the great lion and the serpent.
> "Because He loves me," says the LORD, "I will rescue him;
>> I will protect him, for he acknowledges my name.
> He will call upon me, and I will answer him;
>> I will be with him in trouble,
>> I will deliver him and honor him.
> With long life will I satisfy him
>> and show him my salvation."

We are very proud of our son. He left the United States a boy, and he returned more man than most will ever know. We believe in this cause, and we know that all we have to do for evil to prevail is for good men to do nothing.

Our lives were changed on September 11, 2001; we didn't know how much at the time. I don't know a lot, but what I do know is that this war has to be fought on two fronts. One is along the borders and in the towns overrun by Islamic rebels—that is Dave's war. Without that battle the Taliban will wreak havoc on innocent Muslims, on the surrounding Middle Eastern region, and ultimately on us. The other front is in the Middle Eastern churches and relief agencies where missionaries and humanitarian organizations are working with children who are being actively recruited by terrorist cells. Through Christ's power, we can demonstrate a love that transcends our religion. My prayer is that we will never forget September 11, 2001—nor God's heart for peace on earth and goodwill toward all men.

The Soldier's Psalm continues to protect my son. When he called to say that he was OK (which is how kids often start conversations that include dangerous scenarios), but that he and his fellow troops had been hit by the IED, my mind immediately returned to the psalm: "I'll give you the best of care if you'll only get to know and trust me . . . . I'll rescue you" (v. 15 MSG).

There is more at stake in this war than our attitudes and opinions, more than politics, and more than border control. Sadly, it's a major part of our human experience in this age, and it will continue to be until Jesus's return. Living and loving like Jesus and leaving what Jesus left behind means caring for those touched by war. It means caring for widows and orphans who remain after the casualties of war. It means truly loving those who aim to destroy us.

||||||||||||||||||||||||||||||||||||||||||||||||||||||||||||||||||||||||||||||||||||||

Missional Snapshot

Major Kevin Krackenberger, *a father of two sons and a husband, is serving somewhere in the Middle East as a communications specialist with the U.S. Army.*

With any position in the army comes a considerable amount of responsibility. As executive officer for this battalion, I have ten sites throughout Kuwait and southern Iraq manned by three hundred plus civilians and one hundred plus military. The threat level and amenities vary at each, and my job is to ensure that soldiers have the resources necessary to be successful, while keeping them oriented and motivated on the stated objective.

I came into the job with all the assorted apprehensions and questions. Am I ready? Can I do this? Lord, how do I instill a sense of purpose in others? Lord, help me say and do the right things. Give me the strength and the discipline to do so during the next twelve months, 24/7. As I ask these questions, it hit me—It's not about me. So now I'm starting to think, when I'm tired and don't feel like attending another meeting, it's not about me. When it's 130 plus degrees and I have one hundred pounds of gear on, it's not about me.

It hasn't been easy either. I get up at 0400 [4:00 a.m.] and travel across a couple of countries by air, then complete a convoy to an adjacent camp. I'm tired and really not up to another briefing by one of my lieutenants, but I realize this is important to him. Not only is it important to him, but it is also important to the young private laying his life on the line as my driver. He is driving across some of the most dangerous terrain in the world, wondering whether this will be his last day. I'm also trying to find a balance in eating well, working out, and maintaining my health—both spiritually and physically.

What keeps me going? What causes me to push forward? What draws out the best in me? A little voice inside me reminding, *It's not about me.*

IIIIIIIIIIIIIIIIIIIIIIIIIIIIIIIIIIIIIIIIIIIIIIIIIIIIIIIIIIIIIIIIIIIIIIIIIIIIIIIIIIIIIIIIIIIIII

Something to Think About

1. What are ways you can become more aware and informed as it relates to the war on terror and other atrocities in our world?

2. List those you know who are directly affected by war.

3. How can you live and love like Jesus in relationship to them?

4. What can you do to be a peacemaker in a world filled with war?

"For the Son of Man came to seek and to save what was lost."
—LUKE 19:10

What Does a Missional Follower Look Like in the City?

Tami and I are now officially empty nesters. Our son is in the army, and our daughter recently moved into her own apartment in a different city. It still doesn't seem right that those treasured belongings that once filled the bedroom down the hall are now occupying space in an apartment in the middle of the city.

I rose early the morning after we moved her to her new residence, largely because I had crashed on a sofa hardly designed for sleeping. In the time before my wife and daughter woke, I took the opportunity to explore the area around her little part of the city. I have always loved being in the city—the rhythm of the subway, the glow of the billboards, and the orchestra that rises from a sea of bright yellow taxicabs. What I learned that morning, however, may change the way I feel about the city.

All of a sudden, as I stepped out onto the sidewalk, I found myself seeing the city through another set of lenses: those of a father delivering his baby girl's valuables to a small apartment in a forbidden land. I also began to notice all the darker sides to the city. You don't get as much bang for your buck here ("You're paying *what* to rent this place?"). There was absolutely no place to park; my truck and trailer took up at least three good-sized suburban parking spaces—never mind that they were in a no-parking zone. I figured a $100 parking ticket was a pretty good deal for such a premium spot. And I realized that once Tami and I left, if my daughter needed any kind of assistance, she would be on her own.

I think this city-life thing will take some time for me to get used to. As a father, I often see the city as a collection of diverse lifestyles, some of which I don't necessarily want my little girl exposed to. Then I catch myself wondering if I view the city, as a father, much the same way that I view it as a follower of Jesus: with a wary eye toward those who aren't like me. I wonder what makes me see all these people as so vastly different, and what in the world draws my daughter into such a place? What about the city is so alluring?

I've already addressed the need for belonging in community as part of a new believer's path to finding the Jesus way. This need is nowhere more evident than in the varied collection of lifestyles present in a major city. I think one of the primary attractions that draws people to the city is the promise of community, acceptance, and relationships. Sociologist Ray Oldenburg wrote a book, *The Great Good Place,* in which he talked about the concept of a "third place." The book is built on the premise that our homes are our first places, our offices are our second places, and our third places are somewhere in between, where we congregate and experience meaningful community.

The challenge that Oldenburg's concept addresses is the lack of community we often become accustomed to. The places where we work, live, shop, and play have no continuity and promote no sense of community because they are often separated by great physical distances. The people who live near us are not the same people we see near our offices because the two are miles apart. Consider, then, the fact that our cities often consist of a network of college campuses, parks, storefronts, restaurants, taverns, clubs, and pubs that make up this network of third places.

With this in mind, it makes sense that many of us are drawn to the cities where we seek this kind of community. In the suburbs, where our home areas are clearly delineated from the rest of our lives, we have insulated ourselves from the need for relational integration. For many of us, the occasional morning trip to a coffee shop or café, a retail store, or a restaurant where we are known by name is enough. We have become accustomed to our dysfunction of aloneness and prefer the isolation and noise of our electronics over the chatter of human interaction. Nevertheless, people everywhere yearn for this human connection, and society, as a whole, is looking for this kind of third place where home, work, and leisure all come together. It is the sort of a place where meaning, purpose, and community all come together. Sound appealing?

This perspective helps me understand my daughter's desire to leave the security of her quaint north Georgia college campus for a more lively campus in the city. Here, she will be energized by the concurrent ideals of diversity and oneness. I confess that much of what I have tried to protect her from for nearly twenty years are the very things she has been longing for—the community of a wide variety of perspectives. It is in the city that I am most challenged to live and love like Christ.

As I walked down the street from my daughter's apartment, I noticed a young, athletic-looking couple who had gotten out of their car to walk their dog. Close to a trendy restaurant was a tattered, older man drinking something from a brown paper bag. He was surprisingly friendly and seemed accustomed to conversation with many who passed. I noticed two men walking in the park hand in hand. As I ducked into a coffee shop, I overheard a guru using his summer travels as an opportunity to disciple his followers. In another moment I found myself staring at a middle-aged man wearing a turban who seemed to struggle with the same diversity-induced discomfort I did; he noticed me, and we both looked away awkwardly.

It isn't only suburbanites like me who shy away from venturing outside their insulated existence; sadly, it's the syndrome of many followers of Jesus. To be honest, it's much easier to hang out with people who are like us, people who believe and value the things we believe and value.

If I'm being utterly transparent, I will do nearly anything to avoid the controversy associated with diversity. But Jesus was exactly the opposite—He embraced diversity often in an effort to create controversy. He loved everybody, regardless of social standing, religious preference, or moral conduct. As I reflect on the Jesus of the Gospels, I am convinced that Jesus would fare much better than I do in the city. If becoming a missional follower of Jesus is about living and loving like Him, then I have some work ahead of me with respect to a diversity of lifestyles. Let's examine some of these in depth.

Ethnicity

Serving in my very first ministry position, I found myself working toward the integration of a church in the South as the neighborhoods in that community began to transition from being all-white to including a larger number of African-Americans. The church's children's ministry picked up kids in the neighborhood and brought them to church every week.

One particular Sunday when the regular pastor was gone and I, a young twenty-something pastor, was in charge, the bus picked up the first African-American girl to ever attend our church. By that evening's worship service, there was a buzz in the church about the little girl, and it wasn't positive. Taking my Bible in one hand and leaving one hand free for pointing, I preached a message I called "A New Attitude for Changing Times." Armed with Paul's text from 1 Corinthians 9:21–23, I mounted the podium as a knight would mount his steed and spoke: "When I am with the Gentiles who do not follow the Jewish law, I too live apart from that law so I can bring them to Christ. But I do not ignore the law of God; I obey the law of Christ. When I am with those who are weak, I share their weakness, for I want to bring the weak to Christ. Yes, I try to find common ground with everyone, doing everything I can to save some. I do everything to spread the Good News and share in its blessings" (NLT). I stood my ground in that church, but the church members stood their ground too. I confess things did not work out as I envisioned, as that community of faith was not prepared to hear the message I brought.

Yet here I am nearly twenty-five years later witnessing a similar, albeit less pronounced prejudice. It may be more subtle and it may be directed toward a different group, but the bottom line is there is not a lot of diversity in churches today. Certainly we have the occasional moment when we extend the right hand of fellowship to those who are different from us, welcoming them with our mouths, but if we are brutally honest, we hesitate when it comes to sharing our lives with them, which leaves us far from Christ's example of loving others. As a church we should model the abolishing of prejudice, but, in fact, we have become one of the last strongholds of ethnic purity.

When we look at the life of Jesus, we see the opposite is true. During a discussion Jesus had with a lawyer on the Great Commandment about loving God and loving one's neighbor as oneself, the lawyer tried to trap Jesus with the question "Who is my neighbor?" Jesus shocked him with one of the most controversial responses in Scripture:

"A man was going down from Jerusalem to Jericho,
when he fell into the hands of robbers. They stripped him
of his clothes, beat him and went away, leaving him half
dead. A priest happened to be going down the same road,
and when he saw the man, he passed by on the other side.

So too, a Levite, when he came to the place and saw him,
passed by on the other side. But a Samaritan, as he traveled, came where the man was; and when he saw him,
he took pity on him. He went to him and bandaged his
wounds, pouring on oil and wine. Then he put the man on
his own donkey, took him to an inn and took care of him.
The next day he took out two silver coins and gave them
to the innkeeper. 'Look after him,' he said, 'and when I
return, I will reimburse you for any extra expense you may
have.' Which of these three do you think was a neighbor
to the man who fell into the hands of robbers?" The expert
in the law replied, "The one who had mercy on him." Jesus
told him, "Go and do likewise." (Luke 10:30–37)

On the surface the story is easy to glance through—a tale of
someone who went out of his way to be kind, right? But in truth,
Jesus used this parable to expose how the religious system of His day
was falling short; the priest and the Levite did nothing to help. But
He went a step further in introducing the Samaritan as the example
of what it means to love God and love people. The Samaritan was
of mixed race and was looked down upon by the religious crowds of
Jesus's day, who would go to great lengths to avoid any contact with
this race of people. It is so interesting that Jesus used this example
in relationship to the Great Commandment because, in doing so,
He demonstrated that the neighbor we are to love is not based on
geography, race, religion, or anything other than those whom we
come in contact with throughout our lives.

This has huge implications for those committed to becoming
missional followers because it implies that we are to live with and
love those who are different from us in the same way that Jesus did.
When this happens, it is not unusual to see people of different races,
nationalities, religions, and economic strata working hand in hand
for the common good of those in need.

Gender

Imagine turning on the TV, opening a book, or reading a magazine or newspaper in which women are completely absent. Imagine an entire culture from which women are explicitly excluded, ignored, and silent—that's the world Jesus lived and loved in. As unlikely and bizarre as that may sound to you, remember that the Nineteenth Amendment to the U.S. Constitution, which gave women the right to vote, wasn't ratified by the states until 1920. I don't have to look back that far—I still remember the day my sister walked into the dining room of our grandparents' home and sat down to enjoy dinner with the men. It was 1972, and even though things have changed considerably since then, that day she was the first woman in our family who dared to invade the patriarchal ranks of the dining room table. I'm not sure what she was intending with her presence, but all I know is that she refused to leave and has been sitting at the head of the table ever since.

This may seem a lighthearted family tradition, but when we consider the atrocities that women face in other parts of the world, it is no laughing matter. And these injustices are not events in history that we can point back to, but they are happening right now. This year. Today. According to the Human Rights Watch, "Millions of women throughout the world live in conditions of abject deprivation of, and attacks against, their fundamental human rights for no other reason than that they are women."[15] More specifically,

> Combatants and their sympathizers in conflicts,
> such as those in Sierra Leone, Kosovo, the Democratic
> Republic of Congo, Afghanistan, and Rwanda, have
> raped women as a weapon of war with near complete
> impunity. Men in Pakistan, South Africa, Peru, Russia
> and Uzbekistan beat women in the home at astounding
> rates. The governments alternatively refuse to intervene

to protect women and punish their batterers or do so haphazardly and in ways that make women feel culpable for the violence. As a direct result of inequalities found in their countries of origin, women from Ukraine, Moldova, Nigeria, the Dominican Republic, Burma and Thailand are bought and sold, trafficked to work in forced prostitution, with insufficient government attention to protect their rights and punish the traffickers. In Guatemala, South Africa and Mexico, women's ability to enter and remain in the work force is obstructed by private employers who use women's reproductive status to exclude them from work by discriminatory employment laws or discriminatory enforcement of the law.[16]

This names several countries and is hardly a comprehensive expression of the status of women globally. I think my wife is right when she says we have no idea what is happening to women around the world, and I would go a step further to say we have no idea what is happening to women in our own communities.

This is not unlike the kind of injustice toward women that Jesus confronted when He lived on this earth. In the Gospels, the mere mention of women is simply amazing, and to refer to them in a positive light is revolutionary. It is so easy for us to read the Gospels through the lenses of our own context, but when we do we miss the radical nature of Jesus's liberating lifestyle. When Jesus came to set the captives free, this certainly included women. The radical nature of truth, revealed in passages like the one found in Luke 8:1–3, is often overlooked: "After this, Jesus traveled about from one town and village to another, proclaiming the good news of the kingdom of God. The Twelve were with him, and also some women who had been cured of evil spirits and diseases: Mary (called Magdalene) from whom seven demons had come out; Joanna the wife of Cuza, the manager of Herod's household; Susanna; and many others. These women were helping to support them out of their own means."

Go ahead and read it for yourself. Note every time Jesus mentioned a woman or women in the sacred text. Consider the profound indications for this in our life and culture. Go a step further. What are the implications of the gospel as it relates to those experiencing atrocities around the world mentioned a few paragraphs above? Do we, as missional follows of Jesus, have a responsibility? Imagine the implications for our world if we, as the church, took seriously the responsibility of being an agent of social justice.

Morality

One of the most arresting descriptions of Jesus in the Gospels is that He was a friend of sinners. Over and over again He is referred to this way. Jesus really loved sinners, and because He loved them, it wasn't unusual for Him to hang out with them for significant spans of time. As a matter of fact, He went out of His way to hang out with them, and they went out of their way to hang out with Him. What a compliment when sinners seek you out! The sad truth, however, is that the opposite is happening today. We who are followers of Jesus often repel sinners, and our churches have become the barrier between sinners and Jesus.

I am always amazed by the story in which Jesus modeled the way to be a friend to sinners:

> Jesus entered Jericho and was passing through. A man was there by the name of Zacchaeus; he was a chief tax collector and was wealthy. He wanted to see who Jesus was, but being a short man he could not, because of the crowd. So he ran ahead and climbed a sycamore-fig tree to see him, since Jesus was coming that way. When Jesus reached the spot, he looked up and said to him, "Zacchaeus, come down immediately. I must stay at your house today." So

he came down at once and welcomed him gladly. All the people saw this and began to mutter, "He has gone to be the guest of a 'sinner.'" . . . Jesus said to him, "Today salvation has come to this house, because this man, too, is a son of Abraham. For the Son of Man came to seek and to save what was lost." (Luke 19:1–7, 9–10)

Why would Jesus put His own reputation at risk by spending time with a person as notorious as Zacchaeus? He explained His reasoning clearly at the end of the passage—Jesus "came to seek and to save what was lost." If we are to live as Jesus lived, we, too, must seek out those sinners. And this means we are not beyond seeking them out where they are and inviting them into where we are. Like Jesus, we must pick up and go to their houses. In going, we may be exposed to many things that make us uncomfortable. We are going to have to leave the comfort of our own secure environment and plant our lives among people outside our churches and religious cultures. Doing so is what being missional is all about. Perhaps this best explains why Jesus's Great Commission includes going.

Sexuality

When it comes to being a missional follower of Jesus, it is with respect to sexual brokenness that I feel we are often ill equipped. Yet at the same time, here is where we have the greatest opportunity to help and encourage both those who are inside the church and, perhaps even more so, those who are outside the church. This must begin by seeing sexual brokenness as sexual brokenness—no longer can we separate heterosexual and homosexual sins. Sin is sin, and living and loving like Jesus means understanding that anything other than His way of living is sin. It has been the practice of Christians for too long to talk about the sins of heterosexuals in one way, but when it comes down to the sins of homosexuals, we lump them into a whole new category. We cannot discriminate between sins.

Jesus loves people of all types of sexual preferences, but that doesn't mean he loves or encourages their sins.

Is that revolutionary to you? If you were to walk into our church on Sunday morning, you might see people who are openly homosexual. That's right. For some reason our church has become a place where gay people feel safe. Our church teaches that sex is to be a special union between man and woman within the context of marriage, but we also teach that Jesus loves all people regardless of where they are on their spiritual journeys. I am especially glad these people have found a place where they can belong and become within our community of believers, and for them belonging and becoming involves dealing with their sexuality. I want more sexually broken people in our church. I want them to come to experience healthy relationships with other followers of Jesus who will love them as Jesus loved. I want them to hear the Scriptures taught with grace and truth and to experience the healing and life change that many in our community of faith have experienced through the power of Christ.

It is not enough to simply invite those with sexual brokenness in; we must go to them. Paul put it this way: "How, then, can they call on the one they have not believed in? And how can they believe in the one of whom they have not heard? And how can they hear without someone preaching to them? And how can they preach unless they are sent? As it is written, 'How beautiful are the feet of those who bring good news!'" (Rom. 10:14–15).

Several years ago I took a group of ministry leaders to San Francisco on Gay Pride Day. Our assignment was to go into the city on a sort of immersion journey and see the city through the eyes of Jesus. We found it more challenging then we expected. It was hard to consider how Jesus might view the people who marched that Saturday, and for some it meant struggling to simply get out of the car. In retrospect, I suppose we could only hope that our churches would be willing to struggle with this and other similar issues. Imagine the impact we would have if we faced this kind of challenge and as followers of Jesus went into our communities and cities and sought to live like Jesus, love like Jesus, and leave what Jesus left behind with all kinds of people.

Jesus's Way with People

Loving others as Jesus loved doesn't mean ignoring sin, or that we agree with everything sinners say and do. The woman described in John 4 in the familiar story of the woman at the well represented someone who had a different opinion of sexuality than Jesus did. In the course of their conversation, Jesus acknowledged that she had lived with five different men and the one she was living with at the time was not her husband. She was the kind of woman others didn't associate with because of her brazen lifestyle. Perhaps we wouldn't be proud to know her if she lived in our community today; yet Jesus approached her at the well, asked for water, and struck up a conversation about the deepest issues of her heart and soul.

Jesus was committed to loving this lady. Period. He went out of His way to remove all barriers of communication and relationship. He refused to judge her behavior. He wasn't loving her so that . . . He wasn't loving her in hopes that she would . . . He wasn't loving her to try to get her to . . . He simply loved her. And this was not a one-time occurrence for Jesus, but it was His regular way with people.

In another passage of Scripture, John 8, a woman caught in the very act of adultery was brought before Jesus. Adultery was a sin punishable by death, and the religious leaders of the day knew this and were eager to put Jesus between a rock and a hard place. If He was truly a religious man from God, they thought, surely he would obey the Law. Yet in response to the charges, giving grace and dignity to the accused woman, He challenged those who were the most religious to throw the first stone. From the most religious to the least religious, they all dropped their stones and walked away. Then, the scene changed, as no one was left but Jesus and the woman, standing before Him in the nakedness of her sin. She was alone, ashamed by her exposed body and her sexual act. She was guilty. She had been humiliated by her neighbors. The self-condemnation was overwhelming. She was trapped in her sin, unable to sneak away from the situation.

Jesus was looking down at the ground, drawing something in the sand, but He was nonetheless extremely sensitive to her feelings. Finally, He stood up and looked deeply into her eyes. He asked her, "Where are your accusers?" She responded, "I have none." He looked at her with a gentle smile across His face and spoke softly into her life, "Then neither do I condemn you. Go and sin no more." She left, a changed woman.

I think it is safe to say that Jesus refused to judge those condemned by others. It doesn't mean He agreed with or approved of the sin, but he stood out from the crowd by refusing to condemn. Instead he chose to engage and to love.

A Challenge and an Opportunity

According to David Kinnaman and Gabe Lyons in their book *unChristian,* "The gay issue has become the 'big one,' the negative image most likely to be intertwined with Christianity's reputation. It is also the dimension that most clearly demonstrates the unchristian faith to young people today, surfacing a spate of negative perceptions: judgemental, bigoted, sheltered, right-wingers, hypocritical, insincere and uncaring. Outsiders say our hostility toward gays— not just opposition to homosexual politics and behaviors, but disdain for gay individuals—becomes virtually synonymous with the Christian faith."[17]

While the gay issue is the "big one," it is certainly not the only one, and there are many others that relate to how we are perceived as followers of Jesus and how we relate to other people. It is especially important among a generation of people desperate for authentic community. How can we expect to have influence in our own contexts if we don't know how to relate to a different population? We have challenges ahead of us.

Yet our temptation is to "stay in the car" when we read a chapter like this. It's easy to respond by staying in the suburbs, burying our heads in the sand, and doing our best to avoid Jesus's clear teaching in the Gospels to love others as we love ourselves. Sometimes we keep moving. We know that we should walk across the lobby and introduce ourselves, but frankly it is easier to discuss it in our Bible study group or add an entry to our journal and move on.

Finally, there will be those of us who do something about it. For those of us who are committed to living like Jesus, loving like Jesus, and leaving what Jesus left behind, we will be forced to confront brutal facts about our lives and the utter lack of diversity that's present in our churches and communities of faith. As we rethink our response to our world and specifically people in this world, we will be forced to pray for forgiveness, transformation, and renewal.

Like Jesus, our acceptance of the sinner rather than the sin can go far in having a life-changing impact on others. So, consider your own prejudices and the areas in which you have lost your way. Does your life reflect the diversity Jesus embraced? Does your life reflect a love for everyone He's created? Embrace those who are morally and relationally far from Jesus and help them enter into healthy relationships. Imagine the impact of Jesus's response to the woman about to be stoned—what was intended to entrap Jesus backfired and brought about liberating grace.

|||||||||||||||||||||||||||||||||||||||||||||||||||||||||||||||||||||||||||||||||||||||||

Missional Snapshot

Darrin Patrick *is pastor of The Journey in St. Louis, Missouri, where his church thrives in the city, and a leader in the Acts 29 Network.*

You don't have to look very hard in the Bible to see that God loves cities. As it has been pointed out by numerous scholars, the world began in a garden (Eden), but it will end with a city (the New Jerusalem). City has always been in the heart of God, and so it makes sense that God would want his people to live out the gospel in the city.

Living and ministering in the city bring many unique challenges. For instance, you are forced to be in close proximity with people who don't look like you, act like you, or smell like you. Cities are known for diversity, while suburbs and rural areas tend to be more monoethnic and monocultural. In a real sense, you cannot hide from the "other" when you are in the city.

Our church is located in the same neighborhood where the city's gay pride parade and the local pagan festival occur. Likewise, within five miles of our church, seventy languages are spoken. As followers of Jesus, our church is commanded to love those near us, and in our case, unlike us, as much as we love ourselves.

Diversity puts tremendous pressure on the local church because it is forced from a one-size-fits-all packaged ministry that seems to flourish in other contexts. Diversity demands that the church incarnate in the culture. Our local church is in the heart of an urban center, and we are bombarded with challenges to adjust our ministries and even our worship styles and preferences to reach those who live in our target area. We are constantly asking the questions: "What does contextualized ministry look like in a diverse city?" and "How do we love people who are different from us, as Jesus did?"

|||||||||||||||||||||||||||||||||||||||||||||||||||||||||||||||||||||||||||||||||||||||||

Something to Think About

1. What does it really mean to be a friend of sinners?
2. When it comes to diversity, what are your greatest challenges?
3. What are specific things you can do to expand your relationships to include those who are different from you?

*"I have told you these things, so that in me you may have peace.
In this world you will have trouble. But take heart!
I have overcome the world."*

—JOHN 16:33

What Does a Missional Follower Look Like in Suffering?

Let me get this right," I said. "You're traveling to Emory Hospital for Jane's surgery. Then you're going to Hilton Head for Cathy's graduation. On Thursday night, you're coming back to Columbia and checking into a hotel so you can be at the hospital first thing to have a pacemaker surgically installed. And then on Tuesday, Dad is having surgery and you're going with him." As I reflected on what I had just heard my nearly seventy-year-old mother say (forgive me for rounding up, Mom), I asked her, "What are you going to do after all that?" Immediately I heard her and my dad say in unison, "Go to the beach!"

You would never guess that my mother is being treated for polycythemia, a malignant blood disorder, and certainly not that she has had the disease for nearly twenty years. When she was first diagnosed, the doctor told her that people had lived five to ten years with her form of polycythemia. That actually sounds pretty good when you are fifty years old and in the first year of the disease, but as year one gives way to year ten and beyond, a disease with a ten-year prognosis begins to lay heavily on you, like a life sentence.

The amazing thing is that I have never heard my mother complain. I don't understand it, but she never, ever complains. On one occasion I asked her how she did it, and her response amazed me: "I can live or I can die; I choose life." Her attitude reminds me of one of my favorite verses, in the Gospel of John. It reads, "The thief comes only to steal and kill and destroy; I have come that they may have life, and have it to the full" (10:10).

During the past several years of researching her disease, my mom ran across a clinical trial that a doctor was offering at the M. D. Anderson Cancer Center, a world-renowned research facility at the University of Texas, and the clinic agreed to accept her with a referral from her physician. After one year of this treatment, my mom is in remission for the first time in nearly twenty years. This is certainly not to say that her body hasn't taken a beating over the past twenty years—it has. She continues to fight high blood pressure, irregular heartbeats, and a host of other issues—thus the pacemaker. But even with other physical obstacles, my mom continues to live life to its very fullest, taking advantage of her remission in order to squeeze the most life possible into her years.

So recently she received her pacemaker; a few weeks later she was off to the beach; and before the summer was over, she exhibited at an art show in a local gallery where she teaches art as a volunteer. In between doctors' office visits, caring for her children, volunteering, and serving in her church, she is creating art not only on canvas but in her life every day.

A True Work of Art

About five years ago, things really began to turn south with my mother's disease. She began to experience clotting, a secondary condition related to her illness. I knew that blood clots can really be dangerous, and I was concerned that this downward trend was irreversible. As Christmas approached, I began to think through what I could give my mom for what could have been one of her last Christmases. With a little help from my daughter, I decided to take her to New York City for a vacation. Because of Mom's proclivity for art, I knew this would be a highlight of her life. We began to plan the trip, but her declining health delayed it for nearly a year.

Finally, Mom's health improved, and we spent four incredible days in New York. I had a number of professional responsibilities in the city, and I thought she might enjoy attending a few of the meetings so she could see something about my work and meet people I worked with. I had other meetings planned that would have bored her, so I made sure there were places Mom could go see and things she could do during these times. One of the first days of our trip, I arranged for a taxi to take her to the Metropolitan Art Museum. Like a nervous parent, I called to make sure she had gotten into the Met, only to find out she had been distracted by the filming of a TV show on the street and had not made it inside yet. Later that afternoon, I hurried to pick her up at the museum, only to find her so caught up in the art that I couldn't get her to leave.

My colleagues who met her fell in love with her. The church we worshiped with on Sunday morning begged her to return and spend time there at a later date. The seventy-year-old Jewish man we sat beside during one of the Broadway shows confessed his sins to her. The Ethiopian cab driver talked openly with her about his spiritual struggles and his openness to the Christian faith. Finally, when it was time to get to the airport to catch our flight home, I found myself calling her cell phone saying, "Mom, you've got to get back to the hotel. If we don't leave soon, we'll miss our flight." It was a grand four days and especially poignant for me as I got to see her rare beauty at its best.

The Role of Suffering

God, with all of His artistic expression, really outdid Himself when He created my mom. She is a masterpiece of what it means to be a follower of Jesus, and I can truly say that I don't know of anyone in this world who better models what it means to live like Christ, love like Christ, and leave what Christ left behind than my mom. Still more amazing to me is that she has done all this in the context of her physical and emotional suffering.

It should not surprise us that those who suffer the most tend to be the ones whose character is the most shaped after God's own heart. I am amazed and often angered by those who consume Christianity as if it were a discounted product, while attempting to dance around the real character-shaping circumstances of life. They say they want more meat and they want to go deeper, when what they are really saying is that they want the kind of Christianity that strokes their narcissistic tendency for consumption. Rick Warren got it right when he suggested, "God has a purpose behind every problem. He uses circumstances to develop our character. In fact, He depends more on circumstances to make us like Jesus than He depends on our reading the Bible. The reason is obvious: You face circumstances twenty-four hours a day."[18]

If you are serious about becoming like Christ, and you really want spiritual meat, be prepared to accompany Him on the roller coaster of everyday life and, in particular, through serious bouts of suffering.

Embrace It

Suffering, though certainly not something to get excited about, is a constant theme of life. If you haven't experienced it yet, you will. But before you get depressed, remember that after Jesus warned, "In this world you will have trouble," He was quick to add, "But take heart! I have overcome the world" (John 16:33b). James went as far as to say that we are to approach our suffering with a positive attitude, anticipating positive benefits: "Consider it pure joy, my brothers, whenever you face trials of many kinds" (James 1:2). The apostle Paul added a missional twist to suffering when he suggested a greater purpose behind our suffering: "Praise be to the God and Father of our Lord Jesus Christ, the Father of compassion and the God of all comfort, who comforts us in all our troubles, so that we can comfort those in any trouble with the comfort we ourselves have received from God" (2 Cor. 1:3–4).

I often tell people not to worry about failing God's tests because He will keep giving you the tests until you pass them. Those who live, love, and leave like Jesus understand this, and what's more, they embrace suffering like a good friend. They know that in the midst of suffering life takes on meaning and can establish the most effective missional traction by relating to suffering people in real, practical ways.

Seize the Moment

The most engaging and appealing kinds of people to me are the ones who say, as my mother did, "I can live or die; I choose life." Those kinds of people really get it. They don't measure life based on length or circumstances; they understand that you can exist and never really live. They wake up each day with a renewed sense of purpose, hope, and resolve, and it's not that they don't complain or doubt, but at the end of the day they choose life. Recently I was talking with a young man about his desire to join the army. Because my son is serving in the army, this young man really got my attention. I went on to say, "You know, there is a really good chance that if you enlist you could be sent to Iraq or Afghanistan and you could be injured or killed. It is a really dangerous time to go into the service." But his response was straight to the point: "I would rather be killed for a noble purpose then to live a life that counts for nothing and be killed by a heart attack."

Those who break the discipleship code understand that life is to be lived, not merely endured. They embrace it with purpose and intent, recognizing that hardship and suffering will always be present. Their faith is not based on a spiritual inoculation from challenges, difficulties, illness, or other forms of suffering; on the contrary, they recognize that for life to be fully lived, they must fully give. They drink from the cup handed to them as if they have been in the desert for days without water.

Shortly after he joined the Mountain Lake Church team, our twenty-three-year-old worship leader was diagnosed with leukemia. Rick was a special kind of guy, and I left my previous role to join the Mountain Lake team in part because of the influence of a group of emerging leaders like him. I planned to spend the rest of my life counting him as a friend, with a strong desire to invest greatly in him and watch him grow into one of the greatest worship leaders this side of heaven. I did not know that what I anticipated to happen over a lifetime would take place over a few short weeks in an intensive care unit where Rick lay in a coma. I would like to say it all worked out fine, but it didn't. At least not as I would have it work out. In a matter of a few weeks, Rick had died.

One of the last things Rick did before he slipped into a coma was propose to Suzanne, his sweetheart. They had often talked about marriage and dreamed of a life together, but the proposal was made from a hospital bed that Rick would never leave. I am so glad that Rick and Suzanne had the courage to celebrate their love for each other in spite of such frightening uncertainty. Below is Rick's last journal entry. I think we can learn a lot from courageous people like him and Suzanne.

New life finds me today. With bilirubin soaring to 14 yesterday and back down to 13 there is little comfort, but still God's arms hold me! I'm encouraged when I should not be, knowing that only God's way will work all this out. He'll be the one to say when and where. I would like the role myself right now, but it's a great thing for everyone, including doctors, to have to wait on God's perfect timing for me. . . . That is a miracle. So I rejoice today—with a guitar, a treadmill, and lots of high school friends who realized we all care at some point! Today was a good day. "My soul finds rest in God alone; my salvation comes from him. He alone is my rock and my salvation; he is my fortress, I will never be shaken" (Ps. 62:1–2).

Shortly after this entry, Rick fell into a coma from which he did not recover.

What Those Who Suffer Know

The trials and obstacles that come before those who suffer are often proved to be life's—and God's—most effective lessons. In my pastoral experience, I have learned much from those young and old who undergo such seemingly unnecessary suffering.

There Is More at Stake than Their Own Comfort

There are times in a battle when you really want to give up. I have certainly experienced this temptation and have seen it in those who struggle the most. It is often expressed in terms such as, "I'm really tired," "I don't know if I can keep going," "I wish this were over," and "I hope it's worth it when it's all done." This was even true for my mom, who, in the midst of being severely weakened by her disease, had to make regular trips to M. D. Anderson for her treatment. However, at the end of the day, she has found resolve in her understanding that there is more at stake than simply herself. She has come to recognize that if this trial treatment proves to be successful, not only will she be helped, but many others will be helped.

She is now on a mission that will not only extend her life but the lives of many others as well. I can't help but believe that this is how Jesus faced His own suffering, knowing His suffering would give way to life for many.

One of the most amazing stories of suffering in the Bible is that of Joseph, found in Genesis. A brutal season in Joseph's life began when he was sold into slavery by his brothers and later cast into prison by Potiphar, an Egyptian official, for something he did not do. Doesn't suffering often seem unjust? Later, after years of separation from his family and with an opportunity for revenge close at hand, Joseph stood before his brothers with authority over their very lives. When Joseph finally revealed himself to them, they were filled with fear. At this point, Joseph said, "What others have meant for harm, God has intended for good" (Gen. 50:20). This Scripture gives us insight into the fact that through all of Joseph's suffering, he was not only able to keep going, but he excelled in spite of others' cruelty and injustice toward him. Joseph understood that there was more at stake than simply his own comfort—God was working. When we recognize that God is at work in the midst of our suffering, it brings a new perspective to our experiences because we realize we're on a mission to see God's work fulfilled.

Suffering Can Bring Out the Best

I've paid close attention to my dad over the past few years. I've watched the way he has cared for my mother, both at home and when they're traveling for one of her treatments. When I complimented him for his extravagant expression of love and humility, he replied, "When I think of all I put your mom through before I became a Christian, this is the least I can do." I experienced these same kinds of feelings in the months of recovery following my wife's accident. Frankly, it was one of the best times in our marriage because God changed our perspectives during that time, and our world came to life. We saw things we had seldom or never seen before. We became more at peace and entered into a oneness we had yet to experience at such a level.

We discovered that not only did suffering and recovery touch us, but God used it to allow us to influence others. It opened doors to relationships that had grown cold and added a chapter to our life story that others have benefited from reading. It was clear to us that God was doing something in our lives during that time, even in the midst of Tami's pain and my fear. Through her suffering we began to see a whole new world of opportunity. Everywhere we looked God was at work, involved in even the most minute details of our lives.

Suffering Often Makes No Sense

I don't think I'm alone in that I don't understand suffering. I don't understand why good people suffer, with horrible things happening to terrific people every day. I do know, however, that in the midst of suffering I don't have to have all the answers. It's been a long time of learning though. In earlier days I tried to have an answer for nearly everything because I felt it was my responsibility as a follower of Christ. Today, however, being more mature and knowing Jesus at an even more intimate level, I'm comfortable with the more honest answer of "I don't know." What I do know is that Jesus is there to see us through regardless of the type of suffering. I am also discovering that when I am honest about my struggles and my lack of answers, it helps others deal with their uncertainties because it gives them permission not to know it all and simply move forward in faith and trust.

I recognize that there are things I will experience simply because I am human, Satan is real, and bad stuff happens. I don't like it, but it's the way it is. Nevertheless, my faith is not dependent on God bailing me out of any situation that requires a modicum of faith. On the contrary, my faith reminds me that no matter what I go through, God is with me and will care for me. When others who are disconnected from Christ and the church see this in us, they, too, find hope. We don't need to try to make young believers think that acceptance of and love for Christ means the end of suffering, but we do need to help them see that suffering is very often unexplainable.

Strength Follows Suffering

"What doesn't kill you makes you stronger" is one of my wife's favorite sayings, and when it comes to discipleship or becoming a Christ follower, there are places we can go only through suffering. Paul put it this way: "And we know that in all things God works for the good of those who love him" (Rom. 8:28a). Oftentimes, I think we misunderstand this verse because we confuse it with "all things are good," when it actually reads, "all things work together for good." All things are not good. Life and what comes with it can really stink. However, all things can work together for good in our lives. We often stop reading at this verse, but if we continue we gain insight into how this happens: Verse 29 states, "For those God foreknew he also predestined to be conformed to the likeness of his Son, that he might be the firstborn among many brothers." Did you get that? All things work together for good by conforming us to the likeness of Jesus. It is only through suffering and hardship that we can be taken to the depths of where God wants us to go in becoming Christ followers. Sadly, that's the food we seldom want to eat.

Life Is Temporary

I heard someone say that we are not human beings having a spiritual experience, but we are spiritual beings having a human experience. I want to be the first to confess that this is a really difficult truth for me to comprehend. I love life, and I want to live for as long as I can and with as much zest as possible. I don't understand heaven, nor do I understand hell. I see through a glass darkly (though perhaps my glass is darker than some). Although, I feel a responsibility to live my life as long and as well as I can, I also want to leave my affairs in good order (which I believe is a very significant responsibility of followers of Jesus). I want to pour my life into those around me, leaving behind a legacy of missional followers of Jesus after I'm gone.

There is a certain amount of mortality that we must embrace if we are to be fully alive. To have the urgency required to live and love like Christ, I think we have to understand that our time on earth is limited. Not too many years ago I traveled practically every week with my ministry. Even though it may sound morbid, I made it a habit that when I left home for a trip, I left as if I would never return. For me this meant making sure that I never left for a trip without saying everything I needed to say and making sure that all conflict was resolved. If anything ever happened to me or my family, I wanted to ensure that whoever survived would have no regrets.

If you knew that today was your last day on earth, how would you live it? Suffering reminds us of our mortality and forces us back into that mode of living every day to the fullest.

Go for It

Living like Jesus, loving like Jesus, and leaving what Jesus left behind mean being people who live, love, and leave like Him even in the face of suffering. That's what I have seen in my mom and many others, and maybe that is why I am so committed to squeezing every ounce out of life that I can.

Being a follower of Jesus doesn't eliminate the "why" of suffering in our lives; if anything, it gives us permission to ask. And even though God may choose to withhold the answer on this side of heaven, it does bring perspective and purpose into our lives, even when it doesn't make sense. Like my mom, we must choose life. Choosing to live the life God has given us for His full glory is an incredible way to have missional impact. Remember, this is exactly what Jesus did—He faced a certain death, and even though He knew it, He chose to live and love. It's our responsibility as well.

||||||||||||||||||||||||||||||||||||||||||||||||||||||||||||||||||||||||||||||||||||||||||||||||||

Missional Snapshot

Patricia Putman *is an awesome mom, artist, school teacher, pastor's wife, and cancer survivor.*

My husband and I recently returned home from Houston, Texas, marking the second anniversary of my treatment at M. D. Anderson Cancer Center. I was diagnosed in 1992 with polycythemia. From 1992 until 2005, my red cell blood count would rise until I would have to undergo a phlebotomy. I was constantly fatigued and iron deficient from the treatments. In 2005, the doctor indicated that I was coming up on a day when I would enter into the spent phase of my disease when my bone morrow would stop making cells and I would die.

For a brief time I was depressed, but it wasn't long before I was on the Internet searching for a clinical trial. No doubt the Lord led me to the M. D. Anderson Web site, where there was a clinical trial open for polycythemia vera and other myeloproliferative disorders. Through a series of communication and referrals, I became part of the trial. I am now in complete remission, and my doctor has assured me that this trial is about a cure for PV. I believe that it is only a matter of time before I am cured.

It has not been easy. At one point I really wanted to quit. As time passed and I grew stronger, I began to realize that I had to see the trial through to the finish. I came to understand that not only my life depended on the research, but also those in the future who would become sick with polycythemia vera were depending on me and the others in the trial. Now they won't have to fear a disease that had at one time carried a death sentence.

||||||||||||||||||||||||||||||||||||||||||||||||||||||||||||||||||||||||||||||||||||||||||||||||||

Something to Think About

1. Describe a time in your life when God used suffering to accomplish something good.

2. How has choosing life over discouragement allowed you to have a missional impact?

3. Seeing God in our suffering often brings a sense of purpose to our suffering. Describe how you have seen God's purposes in your suffering.

What Does a Missional Follower Look Like in the Classroom?

The first two years of my college education took place among people who were very much like me, but my third and fourth years were a different story. I attended a very well-respected liberal arts school. I was pursuing a psychology degree, and one of my first college experiences took place in a group dynamics class. As psychology majors, we had to take a practical lab in which our class was fashioned after a recovery type group. This was a long time before groups were cool and a regular part of our local churches, so it was a new experience for me. At my first group dynamics class, the professor didn't show up (by design, it turned out) but left the group with an assignment to plan a "get-to-know-you" party. You can imagine what that was like, leaving such an assignment in the hands of a bunch of fraternity boys. As we talked, I think it was somewhere around the kegs and the pole dancing that I decided it was time for me to speak up. I said, "Guys, you don't know me, but I'm a pastor and I'm not sure about the drinking stuff. And by the way, I'm going to call all of your parents and tell them what you are up to." I was joking, of course, in an attempt to knock the edge off, but in reality by this time we were all very uncomfortable. We went on to plan a party that was more like a ladies' tea.

What I thought was a great moral victory I later learned was only round one in my group dynamics class. The group elected a couple of representatives who later went to the professor in an attempt to get me tossed out of the class. My "victory" turned out to be a major defeat. In about thirty minutes I created a barrier that would take all semester to overcome. In hindsight, I am embarrassed by my actions. As I think about how Jesus would have responded, I realize that He would have saved this exchange for a moment down the road after sufficient relationships had been built. Or on the other hand, He would have enjoyed the party, using it as an opportunity to connect with people who were spiritually disconnected.

God did much to teach me about what it means to become a missional follower of Jesus in that particular classroom. At the last meeting of our class, after dinner at our professor's house, our last exercise was to go around to each individual and affirm who they were and their contribution to the group. When it was my turn, some in the group told the story of our first meeting, one I wanted to forget by then. Each one of them went on to talk about what I had come to mean to them. Some called me a rock; some called me a touch of reality; and others expressed kindness, affection, and affirmation. I was blown away. There, I learned the hard way what it means to be a missional follower of Jesus. Through it all I had learned to live and love like Jesus, and love had won the day.

If we are to move outside of our Christian schools and Christian subcultures, we must be prepared to live and love like Jesus in the context of a secular classroom. Seizing the opportunity not to simply survive but thrive within the context of academic studies presents a huge opportunity for missional impact. For me this meant coming to see the Bible through a new set of lenses. This set of lenses magnified Jesus and His ways.

Beyond the King James

Early in life, I thought I understood the Bible, but in reality I knew very little, and I really believe that one of my greatest challenges was that I did not understand how to live like Jesus. I did know a lot about a religious culture, which, in hindsight, was the result of a very narrow interpretation of Scripture. I didn't know what it was like to think for myself and allow the Scriptures to be a guide for my life. My belief in my own religious culture hindered me from really believing the truth of the Bible.

I still remember a very troubling conversation I had with my brother-in-law. He was a very bright guy, and I had my suspicions about whether he really loved Jesus. One thing was for sure: he thought at a much deeper level about things than I did, and I considered this a weakness at the time. I will never forget sitting in his living room and having a conversation about the Bible. We were discussing translations of the Bible, and he suggested that the King James Version might not be the best translation for understanding the original manuscript. I was flabbergasted, thinking that the King James was the original manuscript.

You may find this kind of narrow, limited perspective unusual, if not troubling, but it was a reflection of the culture I lived in when I became a follower of Jesus. I tell this story because I really believe that our limited understanding and tendency to interpret Scripture from the point of our own preferences or beliefs have become a considerable barrier to being a missional follower of Jesus. Your perspective may not be as narrow as mine was, but we all have to overcome religious hurdles related to Scripture. Perhaps you grew up hearing a preacher who took a hard stance on the place of women in the church, or your parents were premillennialists or postmillennialists. Whatever the issue, consider your firmly held beliefs with respect to

Scripture and examine why you believe them before placing your stake in the ground on a biblical issue.

Inspired, Inerrant, Not Always Literal

Dan Kimball addressed these beliefs in his book *They Like Jesus but Not the Church*. He specifically dealt with how our sometimes narrow views of Scripture have driven a wedge between those who follow Jesus and those who are disconnected from Him in a chapter titled "The Church Is Full of Fundamentalists Who Take the Whole Bible Literally." You may, as I did initially, find the title and the whole discussion somewhat disconcerting, but let me encourage you to hang in there with both of us. Kimball served a wake-up call when he said,

> So today when people who like Jesus but not the church hear the term *fundamentalist,* they don't think of people who only believe in the inspiration of Scripture, the divinity of Jesus, the virgin birth, substitutionary atonement, and the bodily resurrection and return of Jesus (definition of fundamentalism). They think of people who are always saying negative things about the world, are anti-gay, take the whole Bible literally, are card-carrying Republicans, are pro-Israel, read end-times novels, and endorse snake handling and fire-and-brimstone preaching. They think of the King James, finger-pointing, teetotaling, vengeful people who credit God for using natural disasters to punish people for sin, and who use Christian jargon and are arrogant and unloving toward anyone but themselves.[19]

Ouch! If you read this quote and think, *What's wrong with that?* you may need to reread the beginning of this book. I realize that this rather sobering description of Christians represents the cloth from which many of us were cut as followers of Jesus, but this is why it is so important we have this discussion in light of the way that Jesus lived and loved and what He left behind.

I am the product of a tradition that prides itself in being a people of the Bible, and I am thankful for this foundation. The staff I now serve with is made up of many pastors in their twenties and thirties, and I am often in conversation with the founding and lead pastor of the church about how appreciative we are that we were grounded in Scripture by our previous training and the denomination we grew up in. We are sometimes concerned for the younger guys who didn't have that same experience, and we seek out ways to help them come to understand the Bible and the essential truths it presents. I wholly believe we are to be people of the Book, and being people of the Book will lead us to be people of the Way. Our challenge is that in our zeal for being people of the Book, we have often overstepped its boundaries and made it something it's not. Like the Pharisees, we have added our own interpretations that have often replaced the Scriptures themselves. At times, we have come across as naive and arrogant to outsiders, allowing our interpretations and attitudes to become barriers between us and those who are disconnected from the church.

At other times we allow our interpretation of Scripture and our zeal to push Jesus right out of the church. I recall one dark moment in my life when a church leader stood up in a church business meeting and yelled, "What does Jesus have to do with it?" Most of us would never intentionally be so blunt, but in reality we have all allowed our views of Scripture to dominate our public conversations, resulting in squeezing out Jesus and His way of living. With that said, let me state here very clearly that I believe the Bible is the inspired Word of God. I have the confidence and trust that the God who raised the dead from their graves, who made blind people see, and whose words changed the weather can also provide us a Bible that is nothing less than a miracle. I have absolute confidence in God's plan and process for providing us His Word, choosing to work through many different people over a number of years. That in itself is a miracle worth noting.

What I don't always have confidence in is our interpretation of the Bible and certain passages that lend themselves to our own interests and preferences. We must resist the temptation to park our brains and His Spirit on the corner when it comes to God's using His Word to speak to us.

I will never forget one of my first assignments in seminary. The professor asked us to read through one of the Gospels and list every time Jesus said that if you believe in Him you were going to heaven, and if you didn't you were going to hell. I couldn't wait to complete this assignment. I quickly read through the assignment with my pen in hand. By the time I completed my reading, I was utterly frustrated—I hadn't found a single instance in that Gospel in which Jesus said believing meant I was going to heaven and not believing meant I was going to hell. Knowing I must have missed something, I reread the Gospel over and over again, reaching the same conclusion.

Finally, when our assignment was due, I noticed that most of the people in the class had neatly typed manuscripts full of Scriptures they had found that related to going to heaven if you believed in Jesus and not going to heaven if you didn't. I didn't turn in anything. I didn't have anything. As a matter of fact, I felt like I might be going to hell because I couldn't complete my assignment.

Later I made an appointment with the professor, feeling guilt-ridden as I sat on the other side of his desk. I told him that I didn't turn in a paper because I didn't have anything to turn in. I described to him how I had read and reread the assignment, but I still didn't have anything. When he told me I was correct, that there wasn't anything, I thought I had misheard him. He explained that he wanted us to learn to think for ourselves. He went on to say that in no way did he want to imply there wasn't a heaven or a hell, but he wanted us to understand it out of Scripture and not simply because someone had imposed it on us. Today, I still believe that Jesus is the one and only way to the Father. I also believe that hell is a real place that separates people from God for eternity, but I believe this because the Bible speaks of both heaven and hell, not because I was handed down a tradition by the church.

Could it be that we have missed the point of Scripture? The Bible is not simply a rule book designed to create a moral code of behavior, nor is it simply a book designed to spell out a religious culture we must adhere to. The central theme of all Scripture is Jesus, and all Scripture must be interpreted through the lens of His life. The Bible is a book that points us to Jesus from cover to cover, and if we are to live like Jesus, love like Jesus, and leave what Jesus left behind, it is necessary to turn to Him for clarity in the Scriptures.

This clarity comes to me in Jesus's confrontation with the religious extremists of His day. His teachings were revolutionary then, and they still are today. In the Sermon on the Mount, Jesus embraced the teachings of the Law and the Prophets when he said, "I have not come to abolish them but to fulfill them. I tell you the truth, until heaven and earth disappear, not the smallest letter, not the least stroke of a pen, will by any means disappear from the Law until everything is accomplished" (Matt. 5:17b–18). As Jesus lived and loved the Scriptures, He also wants us to live and love them. However, He broke many of the traditional interpretations, constantly bringing new light to their meaning, and He still does today. Over and over again He repeated the phrase, "You have heard that it was said" (Matt. 5:21, 27, 33, 38, 43), always followed by a rethinking and a restating of what this law meant in light of His own life on the earth.

Jesus told us He came as the way, the truth, and the life (John 14:6), indicating that all Scripture is to be interpreted and understood through the context of how He lived and loved while He was on earth. If we are not careful, we can easily begin to view Scripture through the lenses of our own religious baggage and traditions, resulting in our picking and choosing what we apply to our lives in a way similar to a dinner buffet: We gorge on what we like and avoid what we might need.

The way of Jesus invites us to embrace all Scripture as His inspired Word. "All Scripture is inspired by God and profitable for teaching, for reproof, for correction, for training in righteousness; so that the man of God may be adequate, equipped for every good work" (2 Tim. 3:17 NASB). Understanding that His divinely inspired Word is subject to undivine interpretation, He invites us to filter our understanding of Scripture through the Gospels in the context of His teaching about the kingdom. Practically speaking, the Old Testament comes to life through the filter of the gospel, just as the Gospels shed light on our understanding of Acts and Paul's epistles. In order to understand Jesus and His ways, we need the whole Bible. Just as the Gospels shed light on the Acts and Epistles, the Acts and Epistles shed light on the Gospels. At the same time, all Scriptures reveal and draw us to Jesus; the interpretation of Scripture that is void of Jesus is void of truth and subject to our own religious whims.

Learn to Listen

Several years ago, I was in San Francisco meeting with some of the brightest leaders in the country. All of them had advanced degrees and taught pastors in graduate school settings. We were together to talk about how we might better equip young leaders in the church today, and I brought a noted leader from the emerging church movement to speak about culture and how our understanding of it might help. We spent most of our time discussing different views of Scripture concerned with how we carried out our mission, and it was very challenging to me to be the leader of this group.

It was obvious that we disagreed, and everyone was pushing hard to have his viewpoint included. Tempers were elevated and voices were raised. Finally, our guest spoke up, obviously frustrated, but at the same time very humble and gentle. He simply said, "You need to learn to listen to one another."

How right he is. We must learn to listen to what the Bible has to say about itself and to listen to the prompting of the Holy Spirit. We need to come to know the truth of the Word—the person of Jesus Christ. And ultimately, we must learn to listen to one another's perspectives.

Open and honest dialogue about Scripture in the context of real life allows us to grow in our understanding of Jesus, but we must not stop here. It is important that we learn to listen to those who are on the outside of Christ and the church as well. One of the most liberating conversations I have ever had came on the heels of a very complex question about the Bible. My response was profound: "I don't know." In return, my friend responded, "You mean you are a pastor and you don't know?" It was this kind of honest dialogue about complex issues that led my friend to a spiritual journey and, ultimately, to Jesus.

Listen to Jesus

We need to go a step further. We don't only need to learn to listen, but more importantly we need to learn to listen to Jesus. Writing this book has been a real journey for me. For me, breaking the discipleship code has become about returning to the centrality of Jesus in my life. Over time I have found myself losing my religion and finding the Jesus way. It has been an amazing journey. I hope by now you can relate. This journey has brought me full circle. I have been reminded of a passage of Scripture that meant a lot to me early in my journey. It stresses the importance of listening to Jesus. It reminds us that we can get so caught up in the good things about Jesus that we miss the very Jesus we follow. Maybe you can relate and be encouraged by Jesus's words:

> "To the angel of the church in Ephesus write: These are the words of him who holds the seven stars in his right hand and walks among the seven golden lampstands: I know your deeds, your hard work and your perseverance. I know that you cannot tolerate wicked men, that you have tested those who claim to be apostles but are not, and have found them false. You have persevered and have endured hardships for my name, and have not grown weary. Yet I hold this against you: You have forsaken your first love. Remember the height from which you have fallen! Repent and do the things you did at first. If you do not repent, I will come to you and remove your lampstand from its place. But you have this in your favor: You hate the practices of the Nicolaitans, which I also hate. He who has an ear, let him hear what the Spirit says to the churches. To him who overcomes, I will give the right to eat from the tree of life, which is in the paradise of God." (Rev. 2:1–7)

The church of Ephesus provides an example of an entire group of followers of Jesus who believed all the right things, did all the right things, but at the same time had lost their love for Jesus. The amazing thing is, they didn't even know it. As I have said, I have found the same thing true for me in my journey of writing this book. My life has been filled with Jesus things, but has my life been filled with Jesus? This is a question we all must ask if we are serious about becoming a missional follower. It is so easy to practice a form of idolatry when it comes to the Bible and even our faith. God knew we would often substitute good things for the very best thing. Even His Ten Commandments reflect this when He began with, "You shall have no other gods before me" (Exod. 20:3).

In the Classroom

Imagine what would happen if we fell in love with the Jesus of the Bible. Imagine if, in falling in love with Jesus, we experienced the liberating freedom that only He can bring to approach the Scriptures again, not as a set of laws designed for controlling our behavior but as the model for living like Him. Imagine if, in our reading, we discovered a Bible that was not written to provide a scientific accounting of Creation but was more interested in drawing us to the Creator of all things, who is sovereign and continuously at work in His creation. Imagine discovering a Jesus through the Scriptures who doesn't give a play-by-play history of all humanity but is more interested in chronicling His redemptive purposes for all of humanity.

Perhaps our challenge is we get so caught up in the things we don't understand that we miss the point of Scripture. God calls us as a missional people to go into the world. The world includes the classroom, the archaeological dig, and the laboratory. Understanding that Jesus is the Truth frees us up to go boldly and graciously to the places we once avoided. Imagine the difference we can make when we proactively inform these conversations.

||||||||||||||||||||||||||||||||||||||||||||||||||||||||||||||||||||||||||||||||||||||||||||

Missional Snapshot

John Richert, Ph.D., *is a marine biologist and church-planting pastor of Discovery Church.*

When I first started grad school, I thought I might be one of those scientists who believed in God and would know enough about evolution that I could strengthen the debate on the side of God. But then I realized that (1) debating is not my gifting, and (2) I'm not sure how effective that is. Certainly, many people come to Christ from the facts, an intellectual understanding. But in the end, the scientists I've seen on their quest for knowledge are the same broken people as you and me—missing love, never been accepted, or tired of truly ignorant Christians who try to tell us that dinosaurs never existed when we have the fossils that fill museums.

I chose to sit through my graduate years, to listen and learn, to observe and relate, and to trust God had a plan for me, even if it wasn't as a debater. In time, I actually found a couple of other Christians in our ecology program, and we all reconciled our beliefs in God and science in different ways. I know I believe in a God who created all things, and He did it in ways that I'll never understand. I know He holds all things in His hands, and He created me.

There are always professors who want Christians banned from campus because they are "nonthinkers," but the majority, when approached in a gracious and respectful manner, want to hear what Christian scientists are doing. I bided my time, became one of my adviser's most respected science students and a key and well-liked employee of the biology class, and now this Christian isn't another ignorant or naive lunatic but a good scientist and worker who thinks there's something to this Christ thing.

||||||||||||||||||||||||||||||||||||||||||||||||||||||||||||||||||||||||||||||||||||||||

Something to Think About

1. Describe what you think Jesus meant by the phrase, "You have heard it said, but I tell you . . ."

2. How can certain interpretations of Scripture hinder us from understanding the truth found in the Bible?

3. Why is it important that we interpret Scripture through the filter of Jesus?

4. How have narrow religious perspectives kept us from missional engagement in the classroom?

5. Why is it important for followers of Jesus to inform the arts and sciences?

> *"Therefore go and make disciples of all nations,*
> *baptizing them in the name of the Father and of the Son*
> *and of the Holy Spirit."*
> —MATTHEW 28:19

What Does a Missional Follower Look Like in a Religious World?

It hit me. We live in a religious world. I was in a plane cruising at thirty thousand feet at around six hundred miles per hour somewhere between Frankfurt and Atlanta. I was headed home after ten days in the Middle East, and in many ways this trip was like going back to my 1970s Bible Belt roots. I had left the secular West and had arrived in the religious East. For the past twenty years I have been addressing issues related to the growing secularism in the West and how we address this, as the church, in post-Christian culture. Now I found myself in a religious world where once again I had to rethink how I engaged culture. Only this time the religion I encountered wasn't one I was already familiar with—it was the fastest-growing religion in the world: Islam.

Once again I was reminded that no matter where you are, when it comes to engaging culture with the gospel, you don't begin with a blank slate. This is why living as Jesus lived is vitally important. Living and loving like Jesus transcend religion and open up a whole new world of opportunities for leaving what Jesus left behind. One night on my trip, we had a late supper with a high-ranking government official. He had invited us to his house even though we had no official business and we were Christians (he and his family were Islamic). The women in the room connected quickly, and it was amazing to watch how fast friendships emerged among all of us. One of the guys in our group began to do card tricks, which got everybody's attention. Another guy broke out a bag of poorly executed magic tricks, yet everyone loved them. Barriers were lowered and bridges were built, resulting in laughter and new friendships.

I couldn't believe what I was witnessing. When I arrived, I didn't know what to do or say, so I chose mostly to keep my mouth shut. I'm glad I did because it was clear very quickly that God had a plan for that evening. Likewise, I think God has another plan for engaging the religious cultures of the world other than the direction we're taking now. God's plan is that the church obeys His Great Commission, but that cannot be accomplished as long as we believe the Great Commission is all about us. We as the church have developed plans, strategies, programs, and methods that are all about our preferences, and we have grown comfortable in our ways. Our approach to fulfilling the Great Commission has become only marginally connected to the very people we are called to reach; thus, I believe we need to rethink our methods of global missions. While none of us would argue that it is our responsibility as the church to go into the world and preach the gospel, the question arises: What does this look like in a world of varying religious cultures?

Rethink Our Responsibility

We can never forget we have a global responsibility. Jesus had the world on His mind when He gave His disciples the Great Commission, His last directive while on earth. He clearly saved the most important for last: "All authority in heaven and on earth has been given to me. Therefore go and make disciples of all nations, baptizing them in the name of the Father and of the Son and of the Holy Spirit, and teaching them to obey everything I have commanded you. And surely I will be with you always, to the very end of the age" (Matt. 28:18–20).

When it comes to the Great Commission, we have a tendency to see it through two sets of lenses: a local one and a global one. With respect to our local lens, we would all admit that it is our responsibility to make disciples within our most immediate circle of influence—our next-door neighbors, families, coworkers, and friends.

But here is the challenge: when it comes to making disciples, we have done a really good job with people who are like us, but we struggle with people who are different. Recently, I had a conversation with a consultant about the number of churches being planted each year in North America. We were discussing why our numbers weren't increasing, and he made an interesting comment. He suggested the reason we weren't planting more churches each year was that we had already reached everyone who was either like us or wanted to be like us. Breaking the discipleship code means accepting the responsibility of reaching out to people who are different.

The other lens is global. We probably all recognize the necessity to take the gospel of Jesus into the far reaches of the planet, but when it comes to fulfilling the Great Commission in the world, many of our churches have delegated the responsibility to vocational pastors called missionaries and other professional organizations. With the exception of a few "Green Beret" Christians who go on an annual mission trip somewhere around the world, the danger is that we leave this responsibility to reach the nations to someone else.

Living and loving like Jesus bring the local and the global lenses together in such a way that it is impossible to have one without the other while truly following the way of Jesus.

I am seeing this happen in our local church as many people are taking global ownership of the Great Commission. As a result, the world is rapidly becoming smaller for them. A few years ago, while a hurricane was bearing down on Jamaica, one of our World Care partners, we would have prayed for the people of that island. Today, we are in communication with our friends there, being sure they have the supplies they need to prepare their homes and churches and trying to meet other needs. We pray for our friends by name, some of us sitting nervously by the TV watching the weather and praying for God's intervention. In the days following, we go and personally attend to their needs because they are our family.

Many have already stepped up to give the rest of their lives to the cause of serving Jesus with this kind of global lens. What a difference it makes when you reexamine your responsibility and take personal ownership for the Great Commission! Living like Jesus, loving like Jesus, and leaving what Jesus left behind mean building schools, training teachers, establishing jobs, putting shoes on the feet of kids, providing medical relief, and bringing the Good News of Jesus to this island in the Caribbean. Building specific global friendships has become the first step to a whole new way of life for our church.

The Church Is the Missionary

Bob Roberts is a pastor and friend from Texas whom God is using in significant ways to call churches as a whole to be missionaries. I owe it to Bob for being a catalyst for my own journey in this area. In his book *Transformation: How Glocal Churches Transform Lives and the World,* he told the story of how this idea of the church becoming the missionary happened: "The question, 'What if the church were the missionary?' was so overwhelming when it came to me, I had to pull off the road. . . . Wasn't the Great Commission given to the local church? What would it look like if missions became a core component of a church?"[20] In other words, what if the church became the missionary?

In going global, one of the most important determinations we make is seeing everything we do locally as a leveraging point for the Great Commission. Over time, this has become clearer to us at Mountain Lake Church. God has enlarged our vision and our hearts for the world, and we really do want to change the world. Our greatest tension is that we know our vision isn't big enough. Our mission to allow God to create an atmosphere in which people can belong in a healthy relationship with God and others begins locally, but it doesn't end there. As we put it, we "belong and become" in order that we might have "greater impact," and we recognize that greater impact is about what happens locally and globally. In this context missions is not something we do haphazardly, but missions means mobilizing the whole of the church to do the whole of the Great Commission. As we do this, over time we have significant impact.

If the church is the missionary, it means casting a "glocal" (the convergence of global and local) vision, leveraging our resources, and removing any barriers that would compete with our going. This is why it is so important that we rethink our churches as we approach our mission. Many of us are so busy "doing church" we have no time to be the church. Taking it a step further and helping those who are followers of Jesus simplify their lives and become more available is key to the church being the missionary.

We Stay

If we were beginning with a blank slate, maybe our planting of the gospel in the context of the world would be fast and sure, but for the gospel to be effective in the world, we must build authentic relationships and win a voice of authority and respect in the community.

Recently, I met with one of the top Christian leaders in a Middle Eastern country. He shared with our group his vision for the gospel and the church, which was utterly compelling to me. I was moved with compassion as I asked him how we might help. But his demeanor changed as he spent twenty minutes telling me that he and his fellow Christians there must depend only on God because many from the West had come and gone, leaving him and his people severely disappointed.

It was difficult for me not to take personal offense, although I'm sure he didn't mean to attack me. I do, however, understand where he was coming from. We have often gone into other countries as the church and, with good intentions, made promises we have not kept. Our tendency is to go but not stay—to go once but not return. The work in these places is often slow, and as Americans we want instant results and quick fixes. We are impulsive and impatient, not understanding the slow pace of life in other countries. Often it takes years to understand the culture and even longer to build relationships. In my trips to this particular country over the past four years, I have seen very limited progress, though I'm sure sometimes my impatience has challenged the seed-sowing process. I've wanted to give up, not fully understanding our role there, and I'm challenged to discern how we are to have impact. It has been unnerving not to be in control of the process, but I believe at last we are beginning to make headway. We are learning about the time it takes to build relationships and trust, and we recognize it is going to take years of investment and even hardship to take Jesus into this area.

We Serve

When we live and love as Jesus did and we leave what He left behind, it is required that we fulfill both the Great Commandment and the Great Commission. Living and loving as Jesus lived and loved gives credibility to the gospel—it's not enough to tell people Jesus loves you and He died for you. We must die to ourselves in service to them so that they experience the gospel in action through our simple acts of service. To make a difference in many of the religious areas of our world means serving them for years before we see the fruit of our labor.

Sadly, and perhaps convictingly, this is in many ways exactly what terrorists have done with Islam. They have made promises of improvements and often delivered, winning the favor of the local people. This has happened in places like Lebanon with the Hezbollah and in Afghanistan with the Taliban. Far gone are the days in which we were the only missionaries, but today we are the only missionaries who bring the Truth.

There is only one thing worse than the church staying silent, and that is for it to speak and not deliver. As the church, we must find ways to serve people in other places who embrace other religions, and our service must be unconditional. If we serve only those who are easy to serve, we do nothing to further the gospel. Service gives credibility to our words, exactly as earning the right to speak takes time, so therefore we must stay. We can best serve by staying.

We Confess

As we approach the nations of the world, we must begin on our knees. If you take a backward glance at our Christian history, you will see what I mean; we have more than our share of skeletons in the closet. Some of the most widely recognized movements in history were events associated with Christianity, such as the Crusades and the Spanish Inquisition, to name only a couple. Christianity, as a movement, has its dark moments in history, more than I care to remember. However, even as I try to forget, there are many in our country and around the world who struggle with our seemingly religious arrogance.

Certainly this is not to say that Christians haven't accomplished anything good over the past two thousand years; much has been done in Jesus's name that has made way for His kingdom to come on earth as it is in heaven. Christian endeavors have also been much beleaguered; governments and sovereignties have exploited Christianity for their own purposes and profit since Christianity's beginning. There are two sides to every story, and the story we are now living isn't what it always appears to be. We would do well to write a new story.

Donald Miller, in his book *Blue like Jazz,* tells an interesting story of how he and a group of friends set up a reverse confessional booth on their university campus. As intrigued students entered the confessional, Miller and others confessed the sins of the church throughout the ages and asked forgiveness. It had a profound impact on those confessing as well as on those who heard the confessions, and it ultimately opened doors for meaningful dialogue related to being a follower of Jesus on that campus. I envision that similar confessions all across our world would elicit a similar response.

We Lose Our Religion

As I look at the world, it is easy to become overwhelmed. There are millions of people in the country we serve in the Middle East. The majority of them are Muslims, and it is easy to focus on our differences in religion. But to truly impact that nation and to make a difference in the Middle East as a whole, it is essential that we look past differences and focus on living like Jesus and loving like Jesus in the context of the kingdom of heaven. The kingdom of heaven is not something you find in North America or elsewhere in the West—God's kingdom is everywhere. God is sovereign, and He is at work drawing men to Himself. He transcends our religion, our rituals, and our traditions.

When our lives are so characterized by our living and loving like Jesus that people of different cultures notice, we can cast aside our religious self-importance, forming relationships that will lead to conversations. They will begin to ask us to tell them our stories, and our actions based in Truth will lend credibility to our stories.

We Care for Our World

Our church recently changed its traditional missions strategy to a more holistic emphasis on world care. We did it because we felt the concepts and language of traditional missions were a barrier. When someone says, "Hey, you want to go on a mission trip with me?" what do you think of? Many people think of a long trip to another country, requiring that the participant be extraordinarily holy to qualify. Some people think of street preachers in Manila, while others envision dangerously smuggling Bibles into North Korea. Still others think of a trip to an inner-city mission, attempting to hand out leaflets to gang members and prostitutes. Some feel they have to make a vow of poverty and celibacy to go. Many simply don't bother to think about it at all.

Our church decided that the term "World Care" sets us on common ground. We all are called to care for the world, and when it comes to becoming a missional follower of Jesus, we feel this term is more holistic and reflects how Jesus lived and loved when He was on earth. World Care is about caring for God's creation, responding to the injustices of this world, and taking the Good News of Jesus to the nations. World Care means caring for the condition of humankind now and in eternity.

In addition, World Care allows us to invite people we care about to participate, no matter where they are on their spiritual journey. We are not looking for people who are spiritually elite but for people who are open to living and loving like Jesus. This explains why, after a recent trip, three volunteers from our team went public with their commitment to Jesus and were baptized.

Perhaps we're called to care for the world as we go into it, making disciples and preaching the gospel. I mean caring for the world with no agenda, only with a commitment to live like Jesus and love like Jesus. I want to develop a relationship with the Islamic official

I mentioned in the opening paragraphs of this chapter, understanding his concerns, needs, hopes, and dreams; I want to be able to address them in ways beyond a ten-day pseudovacation. I want to build a relationship around a Jesus-like love that refuses to let our religious differences and preferences stand in the way of God's work. I think these kinds of relationships can really happen because for a few minutes, over a few card tricks and a few silly magic tricks, they did.

|||||||||||||||||||||||||||||||||||||||||||||||||||||||||||||||||||||||||||||||||||||||||||||||||||||

Missional Snapshot

Larry McCrary *is now living in Europe with his family, planting churches among people who are both religious and secular.*

For the last few years each Tuesday afternoon, I have had coffee with one of my good friends in a country in western Europe. We often talk about news, sports, and weather. When you are learning a new language, it sometimes helps to keep the conversation simple. One day I stepped out and asked a spiritual question. The reply I got from my good friend was, "I'm not a spiritual person, but I am Catholic."

Our family has lived overseas for the past six years in a country that is deeply religious, where 99 percent of the people profess a religious identity, but only 8 percent participate in any religious activity. One of the first questions we tried to address as a family was how we could take the gospel to a place that is so religious yet secular at the same time. While we are living in an "open" country, we find that the people are nonreceptive to the gospel and our traditional ways.

As we embarked on this journey, I will be the first to admit I needed to reprogram myself on the way I lived my life. We went to the Scriptures and rediscovered the teachings of Jesus and saw how He lived His life on this earth. We had to reread His teachings about this way of life. Jesus also lived in a religious culture, and the people He often ran into were all about the traditions of the religion but not about the relationship they had with His Father. I am on a journey in which I am trying to live my life in such a way that the love and expressions of my faith, on a daily basis, encourage others to look at Jesus. No matter where I am or what I am doing, I want to be salt and light. As I do, I continue to have conversations with my café friend.

||||||||||||||||||||||||||||||||||||||||||||||||||||||||||||||||||||||||||||||||||||||||

Something to Think About

1. What does it mean for the church to be the missionary?

2. How can you as an individual and as a church care for the world more holistically?

3. What are some things we need to confess as the church if we are going to make a difference in the world?

4. How do the Great Commission and the Great Commandment work hand in hand toward greater impact?

*"Let the little children come to me, and do not hinder them,
for the kingdom of heaven belongs to such as these."*
—MATTHEW 19:14

What Does a Missional Follower Look Like in the Home?

I felt a lump form in my throat as I chatted with my son online from Afghanistan. He was updating me on the latest changes in his military life, and even without the explicit mention of it, I was constantly reminded he was considered a high-priority target. For the first few months in Afghanistan, he had been assigned to work inside headquarters, meaning he was working mostly behind the scenes, keeping up with the troops out conducting operational missions. On occasion he would go out into the field, but for the most part he was somewhat safe in an office.

For a while I heard from him almost daily, and I was very thankful for modern technology. How amazing that he could be in one of the most remote places in the world and still be able to connect to another person via the Internet. However, on this occasion it had been several days since I had last heard from him. To be honest, I was getting nervous; but one morning as I worked, he sent me a brief instant message. I could sense the adrenaline in our conversation even before he told me that he had recently come back from a mission. I asked him how it compared with headquarters and was not altogether surprised when he replied, "Ten times better." As we ended our conversation, he explained that he was headed out on another mission and would be out of touch for seven days. I asked him what he would be doing, and his reply came back, "Top secret." Seven days turned into four weeks, but finally he called, telling us that he was back only to prepare to leave again. It was again, "Top secret."

On one occasion he called after a firefight, describing it as hectic and not really wanting to talk about it. Another time he called after spending five days on a mountain at twenty-five hundred meters' elevation, running a reconnaissance operation. At one point I got an e-mail from him telling me that he had a few moments before presenting a fire plan to the command sergeant, the major command sergeant, and the captain of the troop. I swallowed hard as I realized that he would also be the one to execute that fire plan. The day he called to tell us he'd been hit by an IED, he explained, "You may be getting a call from someone from the government, but I wanted you to hear it from me first; I'm OK."

I wanted my son to come home. Soon he would go for about a month to a new place that the army has very little information on, and very little presence in the area. I read between the lines, though, and I confess I was afraid. I was afraid that he wouldn't make it back. I pray for him every day, and for peace on earth and goodwill toward all men. But as I wrote this chapter, I simply waited for another call.

Resist the Temptation to Overprotect

There is a fierce protective instinct within all parents that longs for our children to be safe. At the same time, we must wrestle with the thing that draws our children into a sense of adventure, excitement, thrill, and even danger. We all want to be difference makers, living our lives with meaning and purpose. We know this; yet when it comes to our children, we will go to great lengths to keep them safe.

I still remember conversations I had about kids before I had kids. Truthfully, I didn't know whether I really wanted them. I recognized that this world was unsafe and evil, and I wasn't sure I wanted the responsibility of raising children in such a dangerous world. On one occasion my oldest sister made a comment to me, and I couldn't let go of it: "David, if we don't have children, where will our Christian influence go?" This was the first time anyone had raised the issue of having children as it related to my Christian responsibility or any way connected to missional living. After that conversation, Tami and I began to pray for God to give us children, and it wasn't very long before she was pregnant. Each day of her pregnancy we would kneel and pray for our unborn child. I wanted a son, and I can specifically remember praying for a warrior who would fight for God. Little did I know that God would answer my prayer so exactly.

Obviously, it's not merely the war zone that is unsafe. I have a friend whose son is serving as a missionary in the Sudan and is at great risk. I work with church planters who are moving their young families into the inner city and other similar places that can often be very dangerous. Even the suburbs and rural areas aren't safe— consider places like Littleton, Colorado, and Waco, Texas.

This world is a dangerous place, but how are we going to respond to this danger with respect to our children? Are we going to keep them safe from the world by creating a religious subculture and keeping them in a bubble, or are we going to raise children who embrace danger as a part of being followers of Jesus? Unfortunately, our response has often been to create a safe environment in which we send our kids to Christian schools, allow them to hang out only with Christian friends, watch Christian movies, read Christian books, go to Christian camps, and play sports in Christian leagues. So much for being missional!

Right after Ed Stetzer and I released *Breaking the Missional Code,* I ran across a mother who was blogging about our book.

I loved her spirit—she referred to herself as the "Missional Mom" and applied our book to raising missional kids. Certainly, we didn't write the book to be a parenting manual, but I think she might be onto something. Why not teach our children to be missional by allowing them to be in the world, outside that Christian bubble?

Jesus reminded us in Mark 10 how important it is to remove all the barriers to bringing our children to Him. We have such a strong tendency to protect our children that we often hinder them from living real life. Yet this very thing was happening in front of Jesus, which left Him, as the text says, indignant. He said to His disciples, "Let the little children come to me, and do not hinder them, for the kingdom of God belongs to such as these. I tell you the truth, anyone who will not receive the kingdom of God like a little child will never enter it" (vv. 14–15). Admittedly, I find that sometimes I have been the greatest barrier for my children.

When it comes to raising missional children, I would love to be able to say that I did it all right, but that's not true. I would love to say I have no regrets, but once again that's not true. Our intentions are good, but often our desire to keep them safe backfires. Look at my son: If anything I was overprotective. I never shot a gun with him or even had one in the house, but now he operates big guns for a living. In our attempt to live like Jesus, love like Jesus, and leave what Jesus left behind, it is imperative that we consider our most obvious opportunity to make disciples: our children.

Let Go

When my children were little, my younger sister lost a two-year-old son. It was tragically and shockingly fast: on Friday he was healthy, on Saturday his parents had to cancel his birthday party, and on Monday he was pronounced dead on arrival at the hospital emergency room. Later we learned that he had contracted an infection that quickly ravaged his small body. I can recall walking through this with my kids, who were only slightly older than he was. It was very difficult for all of us, and it's not surprising that it changed my sister's life. But she wasn't the only one; as a result, I held a little too tightly to my kids as they were growing up.

I have often reflected on this, realizing that the secret to a healthy family begins with a healthy me. Most of us have our issues. Some of you are like me, holding too tightly. I heard one mom say recently that there was no way her husband was going to let their daughter go to another country. Let the kids go. Others may be trying to live vicariously through their kids, pushing them to be involved in sports or dance because their parents enjoy those things. Others might be so caught up in their own careers, or perhaps addictions, that they have let their children fend for themselves. The sooner we confront the brutal facts about ourselves, the sooner we begin an intentional journey of becoming better for our children.

Accept that there's more to life than summer camp. Encourage your kids to go to other places in the world and serve people in need; you can even go with them. However, know that you don't have to go far to live and love like Jesus—it could be as simple as going downtown and working with a group of at-risk youth.

Show your kids that it's OK to be friends with people nobody else will speak to—risk your cool by reaching out to these people. Don't automatically tell your children no when they want to do something or go somewhere you wouldn't have wanted to go—consider your motives. Why do you not want them to do it? Is their safety really at risk, or are you merely being overprotective?

Believe me, I know how challenging this can be. I'm living it with my son and my daughter, who moved away to another city. I can be thankful, however, that at least she's independent. I believe it's our job to raise our children to be independent of us but at the same time dependent on God. This means helping them become missional followers of Jesus who live like Jesus, love like Jesus, and leave what Jesus left behind.

Model the Way for Your Kids

I didn't realize how important modeling is until my kids entered their teen years, and their personalities began to really bloom. Talk about the fruit not falling far from the tree—I saw my worst characteristics start showing up in my kids, like my driving habits. I am very aggressive in the car, and my driving is often accompanied by conversations with other drivers, complete with hand gestures (though not any individual fingers). I didn't think much about it as long as no one from my church or religious circle saw me at one of these "better" moments. That is, until my daughter started driving, and I noticed that it wasn't nearly as attractive when my sixteen-year-old used the same gestures and verbal responses I did. Not to mention the nature of the aggressive driving and the cost of a speeding ticket.

On a positive note, we have an incredible opportunity to raise kids who are less into "religion" and more into Jesus. As a matter of fact, I would go a step further and say there is a high probability that if we are more into religion than we are modeling the way of Jesus, they will resist and rebel against that religion. Getting rid of religion for religion's sake and instead following the way of Jesus are our greatest hope for raising missional kids who really live and love like Jesus. I have found in my children that often the religion we most emulate in the church provides very little appeal for them. What they are looking for is something real. This is why the way of Jesus is so much more attractive than a set of culturally religious do's and don'ts. When we go in love to our neighbor, care for our environment, help the homeless, and care for those who are sick as Jesus did, we make a profound impact on our children, who are watching us all the time. They are quick to see the difference between mere formality and the way of Jesus.

One of the practical ways Tami and I tried to model the way when it came to being missional was by getting involved as a family in mission trips designed to care for others. One of my favorite vacations was one we spent in the Northeast with two other families, living and loving a group of kids at a campground. I will never forget the flea-infested hotel or the memories that came with hours of staying outside simply to avoid another bite.

Teach Them to Think Differently

There are two worlds at play. One world is very visible, while the other one is unseen. It is easy to get caught up in the visible one. When I worked with a missions organization, my daughter often traveled with me. One of our favorite places to go together was New York City. We were there often following 9/11, and my role was to help church planters in that city. It is amazing how easy it is to get caught up in the glamour and lights of New York City and miss the invisible world where God is mostly at work; but taking my daughter with me afforded her an invaluable opportunity to see Christ at work even in the rubble, even in the chaos of that huge city. Teaching our children the difference between the glamour and the invisible, in the context of living and loving like Jesus, is crucial in raising missional children.

As a parent, perhaps you've wondered if you had any success in raising missional kids. But there is a point at which you have to hand off the baton as in a relay race. It is out of your hands. Yes, sometimes the baton gets fumbled or dropped, and there are times the race doesn't turn out the way you want it to. At other times your children may seem to run their own races, but I believe this is part of the process. It's not enough to teach and show our children how to become missional followers of Jesus; they have to become that for themselves. Sitting on the sidelines and watching this exchange can be especially challenging, and sometimes you wonder whether you did anything right. But don't give up. It's never too late.

I was encouraged the other day when my daughter called and told me about a church she had visited in her new city. I was encouraged that she had attended a church, and then she went on to tell me that the pastor taught on being missional. One of my favorite topics! She talked with the pastor a few moments later and introduced herself as my daughter. He told her he had just finished reading *Breaking the Missional Code,* which, of course, she thought was pretty cool. I asked her about her experience, and we immediately began to dig into the missional aspects of the church at a level that even most pastors don't go. I was amazed, and for the first time I realized that she was starting to get it.

Lesson of Love

One of the questions I am often asked is how Tami and I have developed the kind of relationship we have with our children. I've had others tell me they hope to have the same kind of relationship with their kids that I have with mine. In the midst of the storms of raising teenagers and young adults, it is sometimes hard to see the calm at the end of it. They are definitely all unique, and they all come with an assorted number of challenges.

We have all had our "moments" as a family. We have felt the pain when our children have made poor choices and lost their way. In many ways we have put our children at risk by choosing to live outside of the comfort and protection of the religious subculture. Yes, maybe we could have done a better job; but at the same time, we live in a real world, and our kids are real people. In raising missional kids, it is important to live and love our children as Jesus does even when we face disappointment or failure with them. I believe the greatest compliment I ever received from one of my kids came from my daughter. She said, "Dad, I love you because I know that no matter what I have done, you still love me." What a lesson: I love you because you love me. We may do a lot of things wrong, but this is one we must get right.

Something I realized a long time ago was that, ultimately, I cannot control the actions or behaviors of others. However, what I can do is control my response. Responding like Jesus is the first step to raising missional kids. When we extend grace and love to them, they learn to extend grace and love to others.

||||||||||||||||||||||||||||||||||||||||||||||||||||||||||||||||||||||||||||||||

Missional Snapshot

Gregg Farah *is a pastor and father raising his children in New York City.*

On Monday, my kids spent time talking to Harry, a neighborhood homeless man. On Wednesday, they stopped to pray for Lisa, a woman who wanders aimlessly through our streets, yelling and screaming at imaginary enemies. Today, my wife told me about the latest "teachable moment." The kids wanted to know why the woman checking out their books at the library had such a deep voice and was named Todd. It's not every day that I wonder whether it would be best to raise children outside of the city. But when talking about transvestites becomes commonplace, the idea can take root.

People often ask me about the expense of living in the city and gasp when they discover my two-bedroom, 950-square-foot apartment costs four times the amount of their four-bedroom, 3,200-square-foot home. And while I would desperately prefer to have more space, I am far more conscious of the cost of raising children in the city. The expense that concerns me is what it would cost to remove my family from such a training ground. Our city provides numerous challenges and prematurely exposes my children to the pain and turmoil of life. But having the chance to immediately debrief the aforementioned scenarios provides an opportunity for on-the-spot mentoring, as we prayerfully seek to develop their character and give them a vision for God's love and care for the people of the world.

We don't have as many parks as I would like, but we do get to try to translate the latest issue of *Hoy!* when riding on the subway. We don't have a backyard for my kids to run in, but we do have more museums and cultural centers than we ever could visit. We don't have pristine school grounds, but we do get to have interesting conversations about why a classmate has two daddies or two mommies.

||||||||||||||||||||||||||||||||||||||||||||||||||||||||||||||||||||||||||||||||||||||||||||

Something to Think About

1. Are you raising your children to play it safe or live dangerously? Explain your answer.

2. What issues in your own life do you need to address in order to raise children who become missional followers of Jesus?

3. What ways can you model how your children can become missional followers of Jesus?

Conclusion

Conclusion seems like a strange word at this point. A conclusion is an ending. For me, *Breaking the Discipleship Code* is anything but a conclusion. In fact, it is a new beginning. When I began this book, I had no idea where this journey would take me. I knew what I wanted to say and how I wanted to say it. However, I had no idea God was going to take me on a journey that would result in my breaking the discipleship code for myself. About halfway through writing this book, I found myself rediscovering the centrality of Jesus in my life. That's right! I'm not sure why or even how. All I know is, God got my attention, and I began to realize how easy it is to have Jesus in my life but not at the very center of my life.

Maybe I rediscovered my love for Jesus because of where I found myself—walking through the grief process with my college-age daughter after the loss of a good friend and getting a phone call from Afghanistan from a son who had survived an explosion while on combat patrol. When you are a parent, both incidents force you to take on Jesus-like qualities—I mean, really taking on the burden of your children for your very own. It was then I realized that writing this book was a real assignment from God. It was a journey of life change for me. One you don't sign up for, but when you get on the other side, you are grateful for the trip. I'm sure the gratitude I feel, and felt at the time, has reminded me of my need for Jesus and

Jesus alone. Writing this book has also reminded me of my need for Jesus and my tendency to leave Him outside the busyness of my everyday life.

However it happened, it happened. I've broken the discipleship code for myself, for now. I'm sure there will come a time in the near future when I will need to do it again. I'm sure I will drift to the left or the right. I'm sure I will inadvertently push Jesus right out of my life. Yet for now I've found Him in a new way.

For me, breaking the discipleship code has been about losing my religion and finding the Jesus way. That's right! I have filled my life with a lot of religious activity and baggage. And now I have returned to my first love—Jesus. I have rediscovered what it means to live like Jesus, love like Jesus, and leave what Jesus left behind. Instead of writing a conclusion, I am writing a new beginning. I am a new creation. I can't wait to see what God has in store for me and for you.

Notes

1. Ed Stetzer and David Putman, *Breaking the Missional Code* (Nashville: B&H Publishing Group, 2006), 50.

2. Joseph R. Myers, *Organic Community: Creating a Place Where People Naturally Connect* (Grand Rapids: Baker Books, 2007), 48.

3. Rick Warren, *The Purpose Driven Life* (Grand Rapids: Zondervan, 2002), 201.

4. blog.christianitytoday.com/outofur/archives/2007/10/willow_ creek_re.html; accessed October 18, 2007.

5. George G. Hunter III, *How to Reach Secular People* (Nashville: Abingdon Press, 1992), 83–85.

6. http://www.thefreedictionary.com/integrity.

7. http://www.cornerstoneconferences.com/pages/page.asp?page _id=17147&articleId=780; accessed July 9, 2007.

8. Alan Hirsch, *The Forgotten Ways* (Grand Rapids: Brazos Press, 2006), 110.

9. David Kinnaman and Gabe Lyons, *unChristian: What a New Generation Really Thinks about Christianity* (Grand Rapids: Baker Books, 2007), 15.

10. Ibid., 155.

11. http://pewresearch.org/pubs/11/mixed-trends-in-religious-tolerance; accessed March 22, 2006.

12. http://www.usatoday.com/news/washington/2005-06-14-christian-right-cover_x.htm; accessed June 14, 2006.

13. Thoughts adapted from http://www.sojo.net/index.cfm?action= magazine.article&issue=soj0502&article=050210, February 2005.

14. Tri Robinson, *Saving God's Green Earth* (Kansas City, MO: Ampelon Publishing, 2006), 2–3.

15. http://hrw.org/women.

16. Ibid.

17. Kinnaman and Lyons, *unChristian,* 92.

18. Warren, *The Purpose Driven Life,* 196.

19. Dan Kimball, *They Like Jesus but Not the Church* (Grand Rapids: Zondervan, 2007), 191.

20. Bob Roberts Jr., *Transformation: How Glocal Churches Transform Lives and the World* (Grand Rapids: Zondervan, 2006), 108.